Continuing the Journey

Continuing the Journey is a four-book series on advanced approaches to teaching English language arts. Written for veteran teachers by Leila Christenbury and Ken Lindblom, the books include "From the Teachers' Lounge," an innovative feature that honors the expertise of both colleagues from the field and highly regarded scholars. Topics addressed in the series include literature and informational texts; authentic writing; language, speaking, and listening; and living the professional life of a veteran teacher.

CONTINUING THE JOURNEY SERIES

Continuing the Journey 3

Becoming a Better Teacher of Language, Speaking, and Listening

Ken Lindblom

Stony Brook University, State University of New York

Leila Christenbury

Virginia Commonwealth University, Richmond

National Council of
Teachers of English

1111 W. Kenyon Road, Urbana, Illinois 61801-1096
www.ncte.org

Staff Editor: Bonny Graham

Interior Design: Ashlee Goodwin

Cover Design: Pat Mayer

NCTE Stock Number: 08642; eStock Number: 08659

ISBN 978-0-8141-0864-2; eISBN 978-0-8141-0865-9

©2019 by the National Council of Teachers of English.

"Cold Snap" by James Hearst reprinted by permission of the University of Northern Iowa Foundation.

It is the policy of NCTE in its journals and other publications to provide a forum for the open discussion of ideas concerning the content and the teaching of English and the language arts. Publicity accorded to any particular point of view does not imply endorsement by the Executive Committee, the Board of Directors, or the membership at large, except in announcements of policy, where such endorsement is clearly specified.

NCTE provides equal employment opportunity (EEO) to all staff members and applicants for employment without regard to race, color, religion, sex, national origin, age, physical, mental or perceived handicap/disability, sexual orientation including gender identity or expression, ancestry, genetic information, marital status, military status, unfavorable discharge from military service, pregnancy, citizenship status, personal appearance, matriculation or political affiliation, or any other protected status under applicable federal, state, and local laws.

Every effort has been made to provide current URLs and email addresses, but because of the rapidly changing nature of the web, some sites and addresses may no longer be accessible.

Library of Congress Control Number: 2019949513

This is for you, Mom—with love—for every time you said,
"Watch your LANGUAGE!" "Don't you dare SPEAK to me that way!"
or "Are you LISTENING to me?!"
—*Ken*

To the beloved memory of my brilliant and passionate English teacher
Larry Duncan (1941–2018), who began and ended his career at Norfolk
(Virginia) Catholic High School. His lifetime dedication to teaching, his
scholarly pursuits, his avid reading, and his selfless work influenced countless
students. Even after 41 years in the classroom, his curiosity never waned, and
his star never dimmed.
—*Leila*

CONTENTS

Foreword

But we *do* language. That may be the measure of our lives.
—Toni Morrison, "The Nobel Lecture in Literature" (106)

Let me begin again.
—Ocean Vuong, *On Earth We Are Briefly Gorgeous: A Novel* (3)

L anguage guides and influences our everyday lives.

We navigate our personal lives and public and social worlds through language arts. We engage with diverse and varied audiences as listeners and also to be heard and understood in conversation. These forms of engagement and expression build our repertoires.

Our use of language can also influence our relationships. For instance, in the epigraphs above, Morrison reminds us about the human need for and use of language, while Vuong notes the possibility of starting anew as we make meaning in and bring understanding to our lives and the lives of others.

A language changes over time and, well, shift happens. As a result, guidelines, rules, and standards are challenged and even redrawn and revised for changing audiences, speakers, and listeners. This applies, of course, to the English language.

In English language arts, rhetorical methods and strategies adapt to new purposes, audiences, or personae. Moreover, diverse cultures and community-led orality influence how we make meaning and interpret the English language in action.

In *Continuing the Journey 3: Becoming a Better Teacher of Language, Speaking, and Listening*, Ken and Leila deliver the insightful stories about language learning and instruction for teachers who are in our communities, schools, colleges, and universities. The voices of teachers and scholars collected in this volume have the power to lift us up in the profession and as we work with our students and colleagues to express ourselves.

We can become more mindful of our practice and the experiences of our students as they *do* language that calls for speaking as well as listening. In our everyday lives, we challenge the limits and possibilities of language in all of our communications.

Leila and Ken confront and address challenging concepts and conversations about *doing* language. These range from practices of inclusion and understanding to forms of exclusion. The language-based matters relevant to our learning, teaching, and responsiveness include articulation, audience, authenticity, bias, boundaries, civility, class, color, correctness, emotion, empathy, error, ethnicity, ethnocentrism, freedom, gender, grammar, humor, inventiveness, justice, media, multilingualism, nuance, orality, performance, play, poise, politics, practicality, punctuation, race, racism, region, research, resistance, respect, rules, schema, sexuality, situation, speech, spelling, standards, style, technology, usage, vernacular, and voice.

"Language is all around us," Ken and Leila declare as we continue the journey with them and beside our students. That we are accompanied by them on the journey, along with the voices we find in the Teachers' Lounge, is comforting and reassuring. In fact, realizations and affirmations unfold in these pages. Leila, Ken, and the Teachers' Lounge scholars beckon and welcome us—regardless of our years in the teaching profession.

Consider the poem "When I Heard the Learn'd Astronomer" by Walt Whitman and the speaker's reaction to the astronomer's lecture and calculations. Like the speaker and Whitman, we readers of this book can gain greater intuition from the examples presented, especially as we move from considering the classroom as solely a laboratory to a space that is also an observatory and a well of imagination and possibility for our teaching.

Because we already *do* language, who can become our teaching guides and mentors? In this book and in the Continuing the Journey series as a whole, count on Ken and Leila to bring us into honest and respectful conversations about language and language arts. They care immensely about us and the work that we do with our students and teaching colleagues. Leila and Ken's wisdom drives us forward to learn and grow—from the 180 school days and yearly semesters into the future. Moreover, their perspectives are insightful, riveting, and powerful.

As English language arts educators, we remain connected to what matters most in our shared work that requires language, literature, and the elements of literacy in action with students in our schools and civic communities. The contributions we bring to language arts education matter significantly as we gain more professional knowledge and continue the journey—rising and soaring in knowledge and commitment.

—R. Joseph Rodríguez

Acknowledgments

As we complete the third book in the Continuing the Journey series, our gratitude to those who support this project also grows. A theme of this series has always been the collective voices and perspectives that NCTE members share, and once again we are pleased that so many colleagues agreed to visit our Ideal Teachers' Lounge. We thank Sydney Bryan, Kelly Byrne Bull, Tricia Ebarvia, Christian Z. Goering, Sharonica Nelson, Molly S. Potas, Kia Jane Richmond, Jana L. Rieck, Martha Sandven, Brian Stzabnik, and Peter S. Willis for stopping by.

We owe great debts to the guidance and leadership of NCTE Executive Director Emily Kirkpatrick and to Kurt Austin and Bonny Graham for their efforts in editing and production. We also appreciate the helpful feedback from NCTE's anonymous peer reviewers. We, Leila and Ken, have both been editors as well as authors, and we can say with confidence and certainty that peer reviewers and editors are critical contributors to every book, even though their names don't appear on the covers.

Finally, we are delighted that *English Journal* coeditor Joseph Rodríguez accepted our invitation to write a foreword to this volume. A passionate and committed teacher-leader, Joseph is insightful and inspiring. We also thank him for his suggestions to improve the manuscript.

Ken thanks Patty for her understanding, perseverance, and loving companionship. Still curious about what drew her to him in the first place, Ken continues to test the boundaries of just how much Patty can take in their *can't-wait-to-see-what-happens-next* relationship. He also acknowledges the support of Stony Brook Department of English Chair Celia Marshik, and Dean of Arts and Sciences Nicole Sampson; their enthusiasm for this project means more than they can probably know. Finally, Ken thanks his mom, Anne Russell, to whom he dedicates this book and who has inspired his interest in language and reminds him that polite discourse is always an option.

Leila is also indebted to the folks at home, both four-footed and two-footed, and she in particular thanks Tucker, who is unfailingly patient and even interested in these topics of teaching and learning. She has dedicated her contribution to this book to Larry Duncan, one of the early and most significant English teachers in her life. In one of her first books, *Making the Journey* (1994), Leila wrote about Mr. Duncan's classes and his work as a drama coach. Even at the age of fifteen, she recognized his genius, and his example has endured. The passage of fifty-five years has not dimmed those memories, and keeping a connection to Mr. Duncan became even more important in his final illness. The two hours Leila spent visiting with him in the late summer before the NCTE Annual Convention were precious, talking reading and teaching and all the wonderful things we can do with Shakespeare. He died shortly after that visit, but his influence shines on. He is missed.

Finally, we thank all of our English teaching colleagues, for whom we write and with whom we commune, converse, and collaborate. Teachers are the engines of the education enterprise, and without them we are going nowhere. We hope this book puts more fuel in your tank!

The Power of Authentic Language, Speaking, and Listening

As you read this sentence, you are breathing. You are taking in air, the blood vessels in your lungs are gathering the oxygen from your breath and distributing it to the rest of your body, and you are exhaling the resulting carbon dioxide that your body can't use. You will do this about 25,000 times today. Even though we have called your attention to this, you will soon forget about it, and you will continue to do it without even thinking.

You could, however, breathe better. You could concentrate on your technique, learning to breathe more deeply and improving your overall health. If you chose to take the trouble, you could do this. Maybe you have. But if you're like most, you haven't.

You just breathe as you do and live your life just fine.

Air is all around us, and yet we generally don't think about it unless there is a reason to: if the air is foul, the air is especially cold or hot, or, in the scariest situations, there is no air to breathe.

In some ways, this is also the fate of language, speaking, and listening. We process the world around us not just using language but *in* language. We speak often, even to ourselves. And we listen (or at least we *hear*) constantly, even if we don't want to. Our ears won't close naturally. You will think, speak, and hear tens of thousands of words today. Yet, even though we have called our attention to this reality, we will soon forget about it again, and we will, in the future, use language, speak, and hear without much conscious thought.

I

We could, however, use language, speak, and listen better. If we chose to take the trouble, we could concentrate on our technique, learning to use these skills more deeply and perhaps improve our lives. If we choose to take the trouble, we could do this. But if we're like many, we won't.

We can live our lives existing in language, speaking what we have to say, and hearing what there is to hear, and live our lives just fine.

Language is all around us, and yet we generally don't think about it unless there is a reason to: if the words are foul, the language is especially hot or cold, or, in the scariest situations, there is no language to use.[1]

As English educators, few of us go through life without paying very close attention to language, speaking, and listening. And we would beg to differ with anyone who suggested that ignoring the significance of language in all its forms would allow us to live "just fine." But how much of our time and energy in English class is devoted to these aspects of the curriculum? Is it truly enough? Are we devoting time and energy proportional to the amount of importance language, speaking, and listening will have in (and *on*) our students' lives? Judging by the numbers of standards and resources generally available in these areas versus those in reading and writing, we think maybe not. And we'd like to see that change.

In this book, the third in NCTE's Continuing the Journey series, we—Leila and Ken—focus on teaching language, speaking, and listening in ways we hope you—the veteran teacher—will find stimulating, enlightening, and energizing. We have chosen this focus because we believe that language, speaking, and listening may not be receiving the attention they deserve in our English language arts (ELA) classrooms, and we trust that this contribution can help rectify the situation.

WHAT DOES IT MEAN TO TEACH LANGUAGE, SPEAKING, AND LISTENING AS A VETERAN ENGLISH TEACHER?

Throughout the Continuing the Journey (CTJ) series, we attempt to approach topics in English from as authentic a standpoint as possible. We eschew highly theoretical rationales for more pragmatic, empirical ends. Thus, we treat language, speaking, and listening in their real-world contexts.

In addition, rather than beginning with highly technical or abstract language about the topics, we start with what students—as people living in a real world with real goals and real futures—will need in order to succeed. Because we live in a rapidly changing world, what students need is the ability to think and communicate effectively and to adapt those skills to rapidly changing circumstances. There may have been a time when there was a canon of knowledge that students could be expected to learn and know. That world disappeared while you were on social media. Now students must be prepared for a future that is uncertain and potentially very different from the one we veteran teachers have lived through.

Teaching language, speaking, and listening as a veteran teacher means, first, that we must teach real, authentic skills and knowledge. We cannot allow standardized exams—which focus on what's easily and cheaply assessable, rather than on what's needed—to dictate what we do in our classrooms. We can't allow publishers, software program developers, politicians, policymakers, administrators, less-informed educators, and other powerful stakeholders to narrow our attention in class to what makes a school, a class, or a student seem to be "high performing." We have to know what our students need for their lives and make sure they learn it.

Second, as veteran teachers, teaching these skills and imparting this knowledge means we must not allow fear or nerves to stop us from doing what we know is important in our classes. Real-world language, speaking, and listening come with a host of serious social, technological, and political problems that some would prefer never to be discussed in an English class. We cannot, however, turn away, as that would not only fail to serve our students, but also be a betrayal of our roles as teachers.

Third, we must publicly advocate for our students' needs and for an appropriate curriculum whenever practical, and we must assist our new, untenured colleagues as they develop the knowledge and confidence to become veterans. Without our support, early career teachers will be tempted to take the easier path to avoid the kinds of instruction—and hard conversations—that we are advocating.

IN THIS BOOK

Continuing the Journey 3: Becoming a Better Teacher of Language, Speaking, and Listening explores the best of our experience, ideas, and research aimed at veteran teachers—our colleagues who are well beyond the first-year jitters and ready to tackle the hard work of educating students appropriately in any circumstance. We are absolutely delighted once again that more than ten veteran teachers have contributed to our book by providing short insights, experiences, and advice in our ideal Teachers' Lounge. One of the most important lessons we have learned and that we share whenever we can is that veteran teachers are themselves great fonts of knowledge. Their voices are essential first ingredients in any work about teaching.

To preview just a bit: Chapter 2, "Language and the Big Issues," gives historical and other contextual information about language and the reasons why we should teach it carefully. Citing newspaper articles, educators' blogs, and research, and drawing on veteran teachers' experiences, we outline why teaching language authentically matters. Chapter 3, "Language Practicalities," focuses more in depth on effective and innovative methods for teaching language, such as avoiding fake rules and focusing on what we call audience-responsive language.

Chapter 4, "Today's Challenges for Speaking," looks at the differences between *speaking* and *talking* and explores reasons for focusing on both, and at how today's technology and social mores have added new complexity to the oral sphere. In Chapter 5, "Speaking in the Classroom," we share ideas for teaching speaking (as both a formal presentation activity and as an informal communicative strategy) in real classrooms. We also delve into a number of tricky instructional situations, including how to coax reluctant students into participating more vocally and what to do when class discussions get heated—as they occasionally will, if we are teaching real-world content.

Chapter 6, "Is Anyone Listening?," is our attempt to address what we consider to be the area of English curricula that suffers the least attention. We examine important differences between *hearing* and *listening*, and we describe ways to teach a range of significant, deep listening skills.

In Chapter 7, "Beyond Your Classroom and Your Students: What Students Need to Know and What They Can Anticipate in Their Futures," we remind ourselves and you—our veteran colleagues—about why we do the difficult, maddening, rewarding, and fun work of teaching language, speaking, and listening, and how that work can reach beyond our time with students in our classrooms.

Throughout the book you will encounter other veteran colleagues as they offer advice and insights in our ideal Teachers' Lounge. And, for the first time in the series, you will find many QR codes, which will bring you to websites and other electronic resources that we believe you will find especially helpful and interesting. Just point your phone at a code using a QR code reader and you'll see exactly what we're referring to. But don't forget to come back to the book!

CONCLUSION

The end of the first chapter is—like the end of any marking period—really just the beginning. We have prepared you, dear readers, for the information, advice, and attitudes you will encounter in this foray into teaching language, speaking, and listening. We hope—as we do throughout the CTJ series—that you find the book helpful, invigorating, and thought-provoking. We also hope you will find it worthy of your time as an accomplished and veteran teacher.

CHAPTER 2

Language and the Big Issues

It's not something most of us signed up for, but at least in the public mind, we English teachers are often charged with protecting and policing the use of language. We are, to a person, expected to know "the rules," the most traditional and strict principles of appropriate usage, spelling, pronunciation, and vocabulary.

We are also often expected to uphold and enforce those rules and to correct (if not condemn) those—especially students, but also nonstudents—who do not conform. The reason for this is clear: for many, the most traditional of English language rules are assumed to be inviolable, long-established norms of language expression—and those who transgress are showing ignorance and disrespect for "the English language."

Thus many in the public see the job of an English teacher as transmitting and enforcing language rules. And this stance has a historical basis. Its roots are deep and, as one scholar notes:

> [There is] a long and complex history of language instruction, including 2,500 years of schooling in Greek and Latin, a thousand-year-plus evolution of modern English from its Anglo-Saxon roots, a growing body of scholarship on that language's diverse origins, several hundred years of broad agreement on "Standard" or "King's" English, a feisty and distinct emerging American English language and literature, a "Latinate" grammar of English created during the Enlightenment, a long history of teaching two of the three Rs in the "grammar" schools, and a century of democratization of American public schooling that had created a demand for mother-tongue instruction. (Tchudi 125)

As language teaching evolved, "the doctrine of correctness" (Leonard) also powerfully emerged, and we as English teachers in the twenty-first century are still grappling with the issue both inside and outside the English teaching profession.

For both citizens and noncitizens of our school communities, the use of variants of language is often an emotional issue since "long-established" language rules can also mean "long-cherished." As overblown as it may seem, acceptance of variants of traditional language can be interpreted by some as evidence of cultural deterioration, of deep erosions of societal norms. For some—and this can include English teachers and nonteachers alike—the use of what many consider "proper" or "correct" language is close to a last bastion of order, outsized in its significance as a marker of civilized discourse and acceptable behavior.

Whew. This is heavy stuff indeed.

It can also be relatively scary stuff, and for some English teachers, the solution is clear. The path of least resistance—and possibly the direct route to approbation—is to accept the role of language guardian, language cop, and in our classrooms and with our students to insist on the most traditional rules of usage, spelling, pronunciation, and vocabulary. Taking this stance puts us on very safe—and well-trod—ground as we reject less traditional uses of language and, by doing so, are also spared dealing with the messy (and even dangerous) territory of language variants and language innovations. Indeed, for some English teachers, the entire controversy is a nonissue, as they believe that their role as language guardian is an appropriate and wholly defensible stance.

TAKING A TRADITIONAL STANCE ON LANGUAGE USE

Accordingly, if we as English teachers take this posture, it means we enforce traditional usage, spelling, pronunciation, and vocabulary principles. What might this mean in practical application? A few examples might help.

It means we discourage the use of a split infinitive (*to quickly run*) and disapprove of a sentence ending with a preposition (*where is that from?*). It encompasses the prohibition of using well-known nouns (such as *impact*) as verbs or adjectives (*it impacted all of us; it was an impactful event*). This also extends to making verbs into nouns (*are you ready for the big reveal?*). Slang and dialect variations are avoided and disallowed in any spoken or written discourse (*I ax her for a pencil; wassup?; can you please carry me home?*). Also out of bounds are recent additions to the language (*bae* or *baeless*), new word combinations (*Brexit; staycation; Cyber Monday; robocar*) and new meanings and variations of established terms (*woke, cold*). Pronunciations are invariable, and when *aluminum* (a LUM i num) becomes *aluminum* (AL u MIN ni um), to take an example of American versus British pronunciation, or *library* (LI brar y) morphs into *library* (LI bry), traditional English teachers often correct their students.

When we as English teachers take this stance, we are often confirmed as educated people who know the rules and are part of an admirable coterie of those who enforce them and the social and cultural strictures they support (as we discuss further in Chapter 2). We also avoid a negative reaction when traditional language values collide, as they often can, with what we perceive to be fair and balanced student evaluation—as Leila's experience that follows shows. Repercussions are no fanciful scenario, and collisions are not confined to teachers who are relatively new to the profession. All of us can encounter this kind of situation, and it is important that we recognize where it comes from and why.

JUST RECENTLY I *was one of a number of readers for a university-based teacher residency program, a program dedicated to recruiting diverse candidates to teach diverse students. I gave a passing grade to one well-argued, timed candidate writing sample essay despite the presence of informal language and a number of common usage errors. Reviewing the scored writing samples, the head of the residency program, herself a veteran high school teacher, told me how "disappointed" she was in the score. Her reaction stemmed from a single source: I had a clear lack of standards. Although the candidate in question was later admitted to the program (there were numerous other*

scored components to the application process), in subsequent years I was no longer asked to be a reader of the timed writing samples. My interpretation of what was acceptable was too broad, too beyond a strict norm of acceptability, to be considered useful.

At the time, I engaged the head of the residency program in a conversation about her reaction, but it was not a positive exchange. Ultimately, however, the timed writing sample was discontinued as part of the residency application process, and I often wonder if the difficulty of scoring it fairly was part of the reason for the change.

This incident is not pleasant to recount. But it does not, by any means, indicate that our only path is one that dictates following a traditional interpretation of language.

To be an effective English teacher and to hold the enviable position of a veteran with years of experience and knowledge, we cannot completely cede to peers, parents, and community members who may be dedicated language purists and, further, who expect us to enforce the same in our classrooms. While many are passionate, especially when they hear or read what they perceive are language errors and faults, we have an important role with our students to play and a dialogue to initiate. Questions we might ask are:

- ▸ Where did these rules come from and why are they often selectively applied?

- ▸ Why must we make room in our English classes for the kinds of new language that are so easily accepted in the world of social media?

- ▸ Why are some variants of language seen as inventive and others, those most directly linked to race and class, labeled as "inferior" or "uneducated"?

- ▸ What happens to our instruction when we interpret language rules more broadly?

We explore some of the answers in the following sections.

THE IMPORTANCE OF LANGUAGE HISTORY AND CONTEXT

As veteran English teachers, part of our job is to bring history and context to the discussion. We cannot be uncritical conduits for inaccurate ideas about language that ignore linguistic research and history. Language scholar Stephen Tchudi reminds us in the centennial history of NCTE:

> There is far more to language learning and teaching than grammar and correctness, and NCTE can be rightly proud of the role its members have played in developing and accommodating research in an astonishing array of language fields, including, but not limited to, language origins, dialects, registers, international and world languages, mass media, political language, social networking and language communities, literacy across the curriculum, second language learning, the social bases of language, and (inter)cultural communication. (160–61)

There can be little argument that some people will continue to find certain kinds of expressions unacceptable and even offensive and certain dialects and accents less or more appealing—and they are certainly free to police their own speech and writing. When the issue is within our classrooms and school communities, however, anyone's value-laden assertion condemning an entire variety of dialect and usage forms is unacceptable and, baldly put, wrong. And you do not have to have a master's degree in linguistics to make this argument with your students—and, possibly, yourself.

SOME SPECIFICS

For instance, without getting too far into the linguistic weeds, the "rules" regarding **split infinitives** and **sentences ending with prepositions** go directly back to the eighteenth-century belief that English should be modeled upon Latin; at the time, English was considered an unruly language and Latin far more rule-governed and logical, even more "proper" of a language. Accordingly, it was determined that the two-word English infinitive (*to love*) must be modified like the one-word Latin infinitive (*amatum*); breaking the infinitive with an adverb (*to wisely love* instead of *to love wisely*) was considered indecorous—and the "rule" was born. Following Latin again, Latin prepositions carry immediately contiguous direct objects; not so in English. But the "rule" dictated that English writers and speakers follow a Latinate model with no sentence ending in a preposition. Following this rule invariably can often be a syntactical stretch, as the waggish saying *this is something up with which I will not put* demonstrates.

Other "rule" issues involve the mainstream nonacceptance of numerous **dialect variations**, again, because for traditional language speakers, their dialect is the acceptable one. Much of this disdain for dialect is exaggerated, especially when we consider that much of the canonical literature of Western civilization regularly employs dialect and expects readers to "translate" and comprehend whole sections of text. Examples can be found in *Adventures of Huckleberry Finn* and other works by Mark Twain, in the writing of Zora Neale Hurston, the poems of Scottish poet Robert Burns, the short stories of American Western writer Bret Harte, and numerous novels of John Steinbeck, including the iconic *The Grapes of Wrath*.

Addressing another of language purists' pet peeves, the **transition of nouns into verbs** (known as denominal verbs, such as *Will you **friend** me*?) and **verbs into nouns** (known as nominalization, such as *This is the **takeaway***) (Clark and Clark), has a long history in language. Indeed, there is little historical evidence that English words are invariably single use. Again, an order is assumed—and enforced in the classroom—that the language itself defies.

This is similar to the issue of **pronunciation**. Despite what many believe, pronunciation of English words is time sensitive and thus variable; there is a reason that dictionaries list pronunciations in the plural, and, indeed, the "winner," or first pronunciation, is not necessarily the "correct" one but, simply, the one that is the most used at the time of the dictionary's printing. It is thus indeed possible that the first pronunciation can shift over time.

New words used in the language, as obnoxious as they may seem to some, are actually part of the long history of English and go back many centuries—Shakespeare himself coined numbers of "new" words (*jaded, rant, scuffle*) and also phrases (*dead as a doornail; vanish into thin air*). Today the custom continues on a megascale: the addition of new words to English is a global movement that has helped catapult English into the *lingua franca* (a seventeenth-century term, by the way, which is routinely used in English) of the world.

One interesting example involves the comedian Stephen Colbert, who coined *truthiness* ("a mere approximation of [truth] . . . unburdened by the factual") in an October 17, 2005, episode of *The Colbert Report* (Zimmer). The word has such resonance and widespread adoption that in 2005 it was named Word of the Year by the American Dialect Society (Zimmer). Although scholars have observed that *truthiness* is a variation of the word *truthy* and is presented in the *Oxford English Dictionary* as rare and dialectical (Johns), the word has real currency in today's era of contentious public discourse, where what constitutes truth is hotly debated.

Who knows these aspects of language? Who will advance this knowledge? The answer must be that we will, veteran English teachers. And, with that knowledge, our students will be able to either split those infinitives or not; make verbs into nouns or refrain from doing so; understand the import of using new words in their writing; and make informed decisions about the context of the language they may choose to use. Otherwise, we set students up to believe there are inviolable categories of right language and wrong language. This is not accurate or, indeed, morally defensible (we talk about these issues in *Continuing the Journey 2*, especially in Chapter 4, where we address "promises and perils" of authentic teaching).

THE BIG ISSUES

From this central disagreement, this ongoing tension between what is considered acceptable in speaking and writing and what is not, stems almost all of the big language issues in English and English teaching. Though we might wish them to go away, they are not possible to ignore. The misinformation we can impart, the intellectual and even psychological damage we can do to our students—or allow to be done to them through our inaction—is huge, and it is essential that as English teachers we assert not a narrow definition but a plurality of language and an informed understanding of language forms and variations. This is the kind of instruction and practical application our students will receive beyond us as they move out of our schools, and we cannot be so blinded as to enforce on them strictures that they will surely be asked to abandon in higher education and in the workplace. If we do so, we saddle our students with misinformation, fuel subconscious and unjustifiable bigotry, and quite possibly set them up for failure in a world that is increasingly diverse and changeable. Our students do not deserve that.

What our students do deserve is a high level of instruction, and veteran teachers must be up to that task. It is not that we adopt a stance of "anything goes," anything new in the language is something we immediately adopt or use. We need to teach traditional rules because students need to know them and the implications of moving away from those rules— and, truly, some of our students will not be interested in breaking those rules. But we cannot simply present definitive language forms and uses without context: we need to teach where those rules come from—the intellectual, social, and political dynamics that created them— and what their variants might be in today's society.

It is, essentially, not an *either/or* discussion but an *and*.

And so in this chapter we move to three of the big issues in the teaching of language: language change, language correctness, and the worldview of language through global English.

BIG ISSUE ONE: LANGUAGE CHANGES

The single most powerful argument against the enforcement of unvarying language rules and prescriptions is the fact that language, over time, changes. This may seem to some as evidence that language deteriorates, but that is not confirmed by history—that is, by the evidence provided us by literature, public discourse, and even art. Language change is clearly evident in our current times through the use and the content of text media, which has, in the past few years around the publication of this series, changed discourse. Twitter, Snapchat, and Instagram (what the kids call "Insta," because *gram* is just so unness, you know?) in particular feature very short snippets of text that often showcase, in their brevity, slang, sentence fragments, and creative punctuation, all effective and widely accepted forms of communication.

If we accept language change—and even a cursory look at sources such as the *Oxford English Dictionary* that provide fascinating histories of words and their variable meanings over time—the discussion regarding what is acceptable can be enriched. We can also demonstrate to students how what is considered acceptable shifts over time. For instance, an audio clip of President Franklin Delano Roosevelt's "Day of Infamy" speech delivered the day after the December 7, 1941, bombing of Pearl Harbor shows students how accent, syntax, and delivery of a formal talk has shifted after eighty years. Comparing that speech to a recorded or video version of any of our recent presidents reveals the change in language and discourse style. To twenty-first-century ears, Roosevelt can sound vaguely British and somewhat stilted; he was, however, an extremely effective speaker of his time.

In a recent position statement, NCTE acknowledges this important issue and, in "Recommendations for Working with Students," suggests that we:

> [f]rame instruction in grammar and usage conventions with ongoing discussion of the inherently dynamic and evolving nature of language, rather than asserting, implicitly or explicitly, that grammar and usage rules are timeless, universal, or absolute. Language shifts; make that part of the classroom conversation. (*Statement on Gender and Language*)

IMPLICATIONS FOR OUR TEACHING

There is nothing out of place in teaching our students traditional, or standardized, language forms and rules. There is, however, everything skewed in leaving students with the impression that these forms are, first of all, immutable, and, second, that they are the only appropriate ways to express oneself. The use of new words, innovative syntax forms, and the consistent ability to be flexible are characteristics of effective speakers and writers. Invariably speaking or writing like someone born decades ago is not the kind of responsible instruction we need to foster in our English classes. We must bring the new into our instruction and show students—and let students show us—how it can be appropriately used and harnessed.

I HAVE BEEN ESPECIALLY *fascinated by language ever since I learned about hypercorrection. I learned, for example, that when people in working-class cultures (such as in the Bronx, my hometown) add an* r *to the end of a word in which it doesn't belong (such as the name* Linda *or the drink* soda*), it may be a result of the person's concerted effort not to drop* rs *at the end of other words (such as* mother *or* center*). The habit of adding the* r*, then, is not a sign of laziness or ignorance (as we were often made to think), but rather may be a sign of someone working too hard to correct some other aspects of language. Thus* hypercorrection.

Language prescriptions are boring and elitist. But descriptive study of language as it actually occurs in the real world is quite fascinating. When my students or I become aware of an unusual word or phrase or grammatical construction, we don't judge it; instead, we examine it. Where is this change coming from? How did it evolve? Why and how is it working?

An example, which at one point had some controversial currency—mostly because it raised the ire of many—is the now widespread, once novel, use of impact *as a verb as well as a noun. Seen for some time as an egregious violation of language etiquette,* impact *impacted everyone. And, for the life of me, I'm still wondering why this one word seemed to touch so many language nerves; even* irregardless*, considered by many a similar language faux pas, never approached the same level of grammatical angst as* impact*. Another interesting one is the recent shift from* based on *to* based off*, as in "That movie is* based off *the book."*

Why is this happening? I've had students work as researchers out in the world, taking field notes as they hear ordinary conversation among

15

people in public spaces. And then we study the interesting results. English is an amazingly adaptable language, and it quickly takes on new concepts, efficiencies, and cultural flair. Even better: when students tune in to the fascinations of language change and development, they also tend to think more carefully about the language they use and when and where different forms of English will be more successful for them.

BIG ISSUE TWO: STUDENTS HAVE THE RIGHT TO THEIR OWN LANGUAGE, AND "CORRECTNESS" MUST BE SUBORDINATED TO LANGUAGE EFFECTIVENESS

Responsible discussions of language also have to include the powerful forces of a "home" language on our students. What we might agree is "standardized English," what scholar Geneva Smitherman has called "the language of wider communication" (Smitherman-Donaldson 170) and certainly the kind of language many assume is suitable for the workplace, is often not the talk our students hear in their communities and from their relatives. When we as English teachers insist that the only right language is standardized "school" language, then we absolutely risk making our instruction irrelevant, even disrespectful and demeaning. Many decades ago, the National Council of Teachers of English passed a crucial resolution on this topic, and the background statement to the resolution notes :

> The history of language indicates that change is one of its constant conditions and, furthermore, that attempts at regulation and the slowing of change have been unsuccessful. . . . Dialect is merely a symptom of change. . . . Diversity of dialects will not degrade language nor hasten deleterious changes. Common sense tells us that if people want to understand one another, they will do so. Experience tells us that we can understand any dialect of English after a reasonably brief exposure to it. And humanity tells us that we should allow . . . [all] the dignity of . . . [their] own way of talking. (*Students' Right* 18)

"Their own way of talking" includes different ways of pronouncing words, use of regional idioms, use of full dialects such as African American English (AAE), and other forms of language variants. Once students are clear that the guiding principle is not an immutable standard of language but, rather, adjusting language to the audience, or what we call "audience-responsive language," then our jobs as English teachers are far easier and more evidence based. For some, home language is nonnegotiable in home settings; a more formal "standardized" language is the same in school and most workplace settings. Regardless, neither home language nor school language is inherently better than the other—and when students are comfortable and assured that their own mother tongue (whether it be a dialect as part of a second language or a regional or cultural variation on their first language of English) has a place, our job is far easier—and, again, more evidence based.

As teachers we have to be aware—and help our students be aware—of the many "Englishes" in students' lives. This is not simply a minor matter of courtesy. As a recent research study conducted in Philadelphia confirms, when we fail to understand one another's language, serious implications can result (Eligon). In particular, this study looked at the transcription of defendants' testimony in a court of law and found that errors in transcription were not minimal but did, in fact, change the meaning and interpretation of sworn testimony. The issue is language, and in this case, court reporters' consistent misinterpretation—if not ignorance—of another dialect (in this case, AAE).

The report details that in the study, twenty-seven Philadelphia court reporters were asked to transcribe for "accuracy and comprehension"; 40 percent had errors; 67 percent were inaccurate; 11 percent were termed "gibberish" (Owens). The consequences are huge:

> Researchers played audio recordings of a series of sentences spoken in African-American English and asked 27 stenographers who work in courthouses in Philadelphia to transcribe them. On average, the reporters made errors in two out of every five sentences, according to the study.
>
> The findings could have far-reaching consequences, as errors or misinterpretations in courtroom transcripts can influence the official court record in ways that are harmful to defendants, researchers and lawyers said. . . .

17

While Pennsylvania court reporters must score 95 percent accurate on tests in order to be certified, the reporters in this study were fully accurate, on average, on just 59.5 percent of the sentences.

Black court reporters who participated in the study made errors in transcribing at roughly the same rate as their white peers.

All of the reporters, in addition to transcribing, were asked to paraphrase what was being said in each sentence. Here, the results were even worse than the transcriptions, with reporters correctly paraphrasing the sentences about 33 percent of the time. (Eligon)

While some of the sentences are straightforward and not truly open to misinterpretation (such as the original *He a delivery man,* which translates into standardized English as *He's a delivery man*), others can be more complex. For instance, *He don't be in this neighborhood* translates as *He isn't usually in this neighborhood*; *I been went there* means *I went there a long time ago*. Misapprehending statements of this sort can result in negative and unintended consequences, and this is extraordinarily serious for the individuals who face court charges.

These issues were also made central at a recent meeting of NCTE college writing teachers. In his remarkably confrontational and yet intentionally "loving" (his word) Chair's Address at the 2019 Conference on College Composition and Communication, Asao B. Inoue charged all US language teachers with building a "steel cage of white language supremacy" by enforcing language rules constructed by White people. He wasn't speaking exclusively of White teachers, but of all teachers who teach standardized English as if it is a superior form of English. Inoue described how using "a single standard to grade your students' languaging [is an engagement] in racism. You actively promote white language supremacy, which is the handmaiden to white bias in the world." Students of color come to class with rich language awareness and conventions that are not truly valued in what Inoue calls the "marketplace," borrowing from the work of Pierre Bourdieu. He suggests, for example, that if we teach that all students must conform to standardized English to be successful in a job interview or in a public forum or in any professional setting, then we are privileging White English and perpetuating its supremacy. Some may recommend that students learn to code-switch between their "home" and "school" languages, he says, but we can't escape the fact that "school" language always looks and sounds much more like the languaging of communities of Whites than of communities of people of color.

We—Ken and Leila—find these bitter pills to swallow. We have worked hard throughout our entire careers to push hard against bigotry, including racism. But we hear Inoue's point that standardized English is based on the habits of one culture (upper-class White culture) and that enforcing that one version of English as the most powerful version simultaneously perpetuates an unfair system. It is unpleasant, to put it mildly, that our efforts—even our best intentions—also prop up unfair systems. It's what Inoue calls a "painful paradox": in helping students, we also indoctrinate them into unfair attitudes about language. Although Inoue is speaking to teachers of all races and class backgrounds, he acknowledges that his message may be especially difficult for White teachers to hear. As Robin DiAngelo has explained in her excellent book *White Fragility: Why It's So Hard for White People to Talk about Racism*, most White people for many understandable reasons are likely to bristle at the suggestion that they may not be entirely fair-minded when it comes to race. As White teachers, we try to set aside our own White fragility well enough to understand that by teaching standardized English as a superior or more powerful language than other forms of English, we may also be empowering racist practice. Inoue understands that well-intentioned White teachers are "damned if they do and damned if they don't." But we can't simply throw up our hands and give up. So what can we do about it?

We suggest several things that we have learned in our last several years of paying attention to antiracist educators:

▸ Learn about antiracism and learn from teachers of antiracist practices. Watch Asao B. Inoue's address—with some colleagues, if possible—and discuss your responses with honesty and open minds. Although it is a community dedicated primarily to literary study, the #DisruptTexts group established by Kimberly Parker, Tricia Ebarvia, Julia Torres, and Lorena Germán is a wealth of information and is itself an example of antiracist teaching practice. Parker, Torres, and Germán also make appearances in the Teachers' Lounge in our *Continuing the Journey 2 (CTJ2)*. Ebarvia has joined us in this text.

▸ Read NCTE's *Statement on Anti-Racism to Support Teaching and Learning.* http://www2.ncte.org/statement/antiracisminteaching/.

▸ Read *Other People's English: Code-Meshing, Code-Switching, and African American Literacy* edited by Vershawn Ashanti Young and colleagues and learn how to incorporate code-meshing pedagogy in your classroom. We also discuss this at length in *CTJ2* (Lindblom and Christenbury 141–52). In addition, be sure to focus students on audience, purpose, and context with assignments that cover a large variety of purposes, audiences, and contexts. Make sure they write often to audiences who use different dialects of English and that they engage issues of importance to communities of different socioeconomic, cultural, and other backgrounds. For example, ask students to write to their relatives, to cultural organizations, to sports fans, to online gamers, to parent-teacher organizations, even to characters in novels. The wider the audiences to whom students write, the greater their cultural proficiency and their writing will become. We are not suggesting that students write in language that is unknown to them (such as White teens writing in African American English); rather, we suggest creating assignments in which all students can write in informal situations to people with whom they are likely to communicate. And let all the students share their writing and reflect together on the differences in grammar, style, and content. In this way, students can learn respect for and understanding of multiple versions of English.

▸ Read (and share with your students) some of the highly regarded books about antiracism, including *How to Be Less Stupid about Race: On Racism, White Supremacy, and the Racial Divide* by Crystal Marie Fleming (2018); *White Fragility: Why It's So Hard for White People to Talk about Racism* by Robin DiAngelo (2018); *Raising Race Questions: Whiteness and Inquiry in Education* by Ali Michael (2015); *So You Want to*

Talk about Race by Ijeoma Oluo (2018); *Why Are All the Black Kids Sitting Together in the Cafeteria? And Other Conversations about Race* by Beverly Daniel Tatum (2017); and *Culturally Responsive Teaching: Theory, Research, and Practice* by Geneva Gay (2018). There are many others. Sharing even just a few powerful paragraphs can open minds and spark valuable learning.

We also suggest that we teachers not abandon the teaching of standardized English as a powerful form of language. To do so would be to impose a wish onto the world, and probably leave our students underprepared. We learn this from the work of Geneva Smitherman and of Lisa Delpit. Delpit's highly influential *Other People's Children: Cultural Conflict in the Classroom* is an important book in which she cautions teachers against making the decision not to educate other people's children in a powerful medium. Instead, she argues that we must teach students that standardized English is a powerful language that privileges certain cultural experience above others. Doing so will be more honest, will be more fair to students of color and working-class students, and will better educate White students.

IMPLICATIONS FOR OUR TEACHING

Awareness of a multiplicity of language forms and how those forms can be effective in different contexts is part of our role as English teachers. When we imply to our students that their own language is deficient and that what they bring into our classroom is not acceptable, we do them a huge disservice not only in our classes but also to their future lives. We also expose our own ignorance about how language works. Presenting our students with a message to impart and then letting them experiment with sending that message to multiple audiences provides an invaluable lesson in how language can be tailored effectively to specific hearers. Audience-responsive language is simply more effective than language that assumes all audiences are the same—or should be. We also must remember that correcting and condemning students' language has broad and damaging effects. This comment (attributed to a number of people but largely credited to Maya Angelou) is appropriate to cite here: "I've learned that people will forget what you said, people will forget what you did, but people will never forget how you made them feel." Condemning and belittling students' language can have far-reaching effects. Opening our classrooms to language variants and exploring, even celebrating, those variants sends a powerful message of inclusion and diversity.

BIG ISSUE THREE: NO ONE CULTURE OWNS THIS LANGUAGE/THE EMERGENCE OF GLOBAL ENGLISH

If there were a great sweepstakes for global language dominance, English has won first prize. "One of the world's great growth industries" (Bryson 13), English as a language continues to expand and add, and it has become the language used most widely in the world. History, economics, and global media explain some of this dominance, but there are other factors also that make English particularly appealing and popular.

This was not always so. Just a few decades ago, the advocacy for knowing at least one other language permeated academic and cultural circles. Now, however, it appears that the interest in mastering a second language has waned in the United States. In early 2019, the Modern Language Association reported a sharp decline in foreign language courses offered in American universities (Johnson), no fewer than 651 foreign language programs closing in a "recent three-year period," from 2013 to 2016. In addition, the required credits in a foreign language have now declined in most college admission criteria, leading to fewer foreign language courses offered in high school. We consider these changes intensely sad in our increasingly complex world. But, others may ask, who needs Spanish, German, or Japanese when English is used almost all over the world? The question may seem arrogant and out of place, showing disrespect for the various cultures and traditions of the globe, but the bald fact is that English is now the dominant worldwide tongue. There are, of course, many *Englishes,* and variations in accent, vocabulary, and pronunciation abound. And English as a universal lingua franca—at least as the language of commerce—continues to grow.

What has contributed to this dominance of English? Again, economics and global media play powerful roles, as does the legacy of colonial domination (such as in India and certain Caribbean and African countries—and don't forget the United States). But some of the appeal of English may well be the language's extreme elasticity, accepting "loan words" from other languages (e.g., *guru* from Sanskrit; *cookie* from Dutch; *safari* from Arabic), incorporating invented words (*podcast, sexting*), letting nouns merge into verbs (*gift, book, keyboard, elbow*) and verbs into nouns (*solve, reveal, ask*), all in an almost delirious mix of communication that can—and does—change on almost a daily basis. And while language purists can lament this aspect of English (as did my local paper in a recent editorial, conveying "our disdain" for the "misappropriation of nouns" and the "verbification that runs rampant today" [*Richmond Times-Dispatch*]), the dirty deeds are regularly done.

With this as a preface, then, it seems that the traditional "gotcha" game—catching people in so-called errors of language—is doubly antique. It's not only an appeal to linguistic snobbery, but it also clearly ignores the power of English and one of the reasons that the language, malleable and plastic, has been adopted so widely across the globe.

IMPLICATIONS FOR OUR TEACHING

If English teachers feel that there are clear and bright lines, boundaries as it were, around English as a language, then those frontiers have shifted markedly. When English speakers come into our classes and hail from different parts of the world, they bring with them a full set of different Englishes. While certainly it has been acceptable to find British speakers quaint ("the United States and Great Britain are two countries separated by a common language," George Bernard Shaw is supposed to have quipped), the difference in Englishes is beyond the pronunciation of *aluminum,* a car's trunk becoming a *boot*, a sweater being a *jumper*, or, from Australia, putting shrimp on the *barbie* (barbeque). The vocabulary, pronunciation, and even syntactical variants of the world's Englishes come into our classrooms on a regular basis. And we need to welcome them and use them.

Speaking of being welcoming, we also need to be supportive of the students who come to our classrooms learning English as a new language. The strategies that work for English language learners (ELLs) are not the same as those that work for native speakers. It is important for us also to remember that ELLs are emergent bilinguals or multilinguals, and their experience with languages can be a significant advantage for them over native English speakers with experience in only one language. Our colleague Kelly Byrne Bull was kind enough to stop by our Teachers' Lounge to tell us about a pedagogical method she finds helpful.

— FROM THE TEACHERS' LOUNGE —

Do We Design Instruction So All Students Can Actively Participate in Discussions?

Kelly Byrne Bull

Notre Dame of Maryland University, Baltimore, Maryland

I've become a big fan of the Sheltered Instruction Observation Protocol (SIOP), which provides English language learners with the support they need to learn content. Using sheltered instruction helps culturally and linguistically diverse learners deepen their understanding of content while improving their English language proficiency. Discussions help to establish positive interactions among students of different national, ethnic, religious, social, or cultural backgrounds. Speaking and listening build foundations for understanding and appreciating different perspectives, which is the heart of the English language arts classroom.

Culturally and linguistically diverse students need built-in support or scaffolding because they are doing double the work, learning the language and the content simultaneously. For me, it's important that I know students' WIDA (https://wida.wisc.edu/) test scores in the domains of listening, speaking, reading, and writing (75 percent of states use the WIDA test). Then I look to WIDA's Can-Do Descriptors, which are designed to help classroom teachers understand what students at different levels of English proficiency should be able to do. These descriptors enable teachers to challenge each student within their current language abilities.

Knowing this information, I design my instruction so that my students have both the tools and the opportunities to be successful in speaking with their peers. Tools include the tangible resources I provide such as illustrations, diagrams, graphic organizers, and sentence frames;

such visual aids provide meaningful language support. Opportunities are the carefully planned instances in which my students have time to think, talk, and reflect. I arrange frequent and varied opportunities for my kids to talk with a partner, in small groups, and in whole-class discussions. When ELLs use visual supports when talking with peers who are fluent English speakers, they can engage in authentic discussions centered on course content.

CONCLUSION

What is the import of this discussion of the big issues and the plea for a broader interpretation and teaching of language and its forms? Why this argument about the importance of language and language forms?[2]

To name is power.

After all, English class exists, as it always has, within the territory of an unjust world. And, while there are stellar exceptions, English class has often served that unjust world fairly well. English class, in the past and in our own twenty-first-century democracy, has often been used to advance political and cultural ends, not all of which are benevolent. Flying under the flag of correctness, assimilation, even intelligibility, English classroom instruction regarding language, regulation of accent, vocabulary, and syntax has had mixed results. Such instruction has ensured that many leave English class confirmed regarding their superiority and their rightful place in the world. In response to that same instruction, many leave English class convinced of their inferiority and lack of fit in the wider society.

This is often no one's heinous and horrid fault: it is the way of the herd, how society ensures that all stay clustered in the group, no stragglers, no outsiders. It is also how we ensure the herd survives, how we transmit and carry on. As noted before, in school, in English class, we teachers are vulnerable to this kind of pressure, and for a variety of reasons some of us cooperate with it. And some of us don't.

Every day, many teachers all over this country know that English class can also be more, and the opportunity to make it more, to open it up, comes at its intersection with our discipline's content and its potent language subtext, the power to call out, to label, to accurately and fairly *name*.

To name is power.

In many creation stories, the deity gives new humans the power to name. The animals and the natural features are then duly labeled and proclaimed: *This is an elephant, this is a cactus, this is a river.* In literature, from the contemporary to the ancient, the protagonist's name is also essential. In numerous epics, the hero's name is hidden until an appropriately dramatic time. In the classics we teach in English, Homer's Odysseus comes home and disguises his name; Arthur Miller's John Proctor fights to defend his. Shakespeare's Juliet wonders if she and Romeo can avoid deadly consequences if only he were called by a different name; in service of his own evil designs, Iago twists the meaning of a "good" name. Sandra Cisneros's Esperanza meditates on the importance of her name and yearns for others to pronounce it correctly. James Baldwin thunders that *nobody knows my name.*

What do we name in English class? The list is countless. We may start with full and just and accurate names for groups. And we explore with our students why we even engage in this discussion. Are some people *Indian, Native American, American Indian,* or *Indigenous?* Should a specific person always be referred to by her tribe, such as *Lakota Sioux?* How does this naming change and evolve, and why? Consider the shifting of acceptable terms from *colored* to *Negro* to *Black, African American,* and also *person of color* (and today, what is the place of the powerful and toxic *n*-word?). Why? Are individuals *Latino (Latinx?)* or *Hispanic?* Are they *Caucasian, White, non-Hispanic White?* What is the history of these terms; does it make a difference, and to whom does it make a difference?

To extend this consideration of terminology beyond race and ethnic identity: Is it *disabled* or a *person with disabilities? A person with autism* or an *autistic person? Temporarily able-bodied, neuro-typical,* or *nondisabled? A slave* or a *person who is enslaved?* Are women *Miss* or *Mrs.* or *Ms.?* Or *Mx.?* Should we call someone a *girl* or *gurl* or *young woman?* (What about *bitch* and *ho?*) *Women* or *females?* Do I wish that you not call me *he* or *she*, but *they?* Do I wrest away the scorn of a term and proclaim that I am *queer*, not *lesbian*, not *homosexual*, not *gay*? *Transgender, gender nonconforming*, or *nonbinary*? What do you assume about me if you call me *Gen X* or *Gen Y* or *Millennial*?

And it extends to the political: Is it *civil disobedience* or *insurrection*? *Murder* or *ethnic cleansing*? *Torture* or *enhanced interrogation*? *Patriotism* or *terrorism*? Does it matter whether we call it *global warming* or *climate change*? Is it a *fact* or *fake news* or an *alternative fact* or just an *outright lie*? Is it *truthy*? In the end, does it make any difference?

In the end, it really, really does make a difference.

Language is powerful. How we and our beliefs are named by others—which then affects how we view ourselves and our actions—is crucial. How we name ourselves and what we believe can empower us and guide our actions. Often there is a gap, a tension, between how others name us and how we name us, and attention to this gap is essential. George Orwell explores the issue with devastating conclusions in his essay "Politics and the English Language," maintaining that when we accept names that are perversions, that are blatant tools of corrupted power, we have subverted reality, we have subverted justice. When we name a thing or individual and insist that that term is the just and accurate one, we uphold our own sense of self and identity. When we name, we control, in certain ways, our own reality, and we invite others to share it. And when we impose our names on the realities of others, we are attempting to control them as well.

The search for equity and fairness is a never-ending one, and while we take heart from Dr. Martin Luther King Jr.'s belief that "the arc of the moral universe is long, but it bends toward justice," it is indeed a long and continual endeavor, and it is enacted all over this country in English classes every day. For us, as conscientious teachers, it is our honor and privilege to explore with our students the just and accurate names, the language that does not obfuscate but that illumines and proclaims, confidently and boldly: This is what it really is. This is the true name.

CHAPTER 3

Language Practicalities

WHICH LANGUAGE WHEN

As teachers we are often ambassadors to the public, and in the realm of language, our expertise is vital. People who do not know much about language are rarely interested in paying much attention to their own use of language. Certainly we cannot send the world back to school to study language origin and use, even if that were desirable, but we can invite people to consider how they, in daily life, show their keen adaptability to the demands of routine discourse interactions. For instance, how someone addresses a person in power surely differs from how they address a peer or someone with whom they are doing business. The drive-through attendant gets a different level of language than the loan officer at the bank; the neighbor's daughter may well be addressed differently than the technician at the nail salon. None of this is terribly high level or insightful, and, truth to tell, most people don't think much about it, but it is part of how almost everyone uses a different flavor of language in a different context.

When Samuel Johnson's eighteenth-century *Dictionary of the English Language* became the language Bible, the standard in English, for the first time certain types of usage in speech and writing became class and even morality markers. For English teachers, who are expected to know and enforce these rules, it is often seen as a "gotcha" correctness game in which the pronunciation and usage of the language is an endless set of hurdles over which only the cognoscenti can leap. Thus, the quest for absolute correctness can be an enemy to the authenticity that we advocate (see our *Continuing the Journey 2: Becoming a Better Teacher of Authentic Writing*); despite what might be our best intentions, the absolute adherence to rigid, immutable language conventions can silence our students and also make our communication with students more an etiquette class than one devoted to clarity, forcefulness, and persuasiveness.

The reason for consistent language adjustment is not hard to unpack: in our speech and in our writing, we use different intonations, vocabulary, and level of complexity depending on context and hearer(s). These differences can be based on the level of formality and familiarity between us and our hearer(s) and based on possible shared cultural backgrounds (in terms of neighborhood we grew up in, professional vocabulary we share, and shorthand phrases and anecdotes we hold in common). And, as we readily understand, even on a subliminal level, if we make a misstep in our language adjustment, we are likely to face a communication misunderstanding or, in extreme conditions, a communication breakdown. Making oneself *heard*—which essentially means making oneself *understood*—is vital to our society and to our success as human beings. In school, in English class, we teachers are part of this communications lesson and learning and, as veterans, we teachers are at the forefront of correcting what are often highly inaccurate—even occasionally laughable—conclusions about the use of language. We are also at the forefront of effective language teaching.

COMMUNICATION AND FAKE RULES ABOUT LANGUAGE

When you first began teaching, it may have been important for you to establish with your students that you indeed did know what a *split infinitive* meant (e.g., *to quickly walk* vs. *to walk quickly*) and to caution your students about its use in formal writing. As we discussed in a previous chapter, not every reader, even sophisticated adult readers, understands the artificiality of this prohibition (based on the Latin origin of the single-word infinitive) and instead assumes that "splitting" the *to* and the *verb* of an infinitive is an error. It is not; the prohibition is fake, a bogus nonrule, what Edgar Schuster called a "myth-rule," and it falls somewhere near the same category of outdated advice as wearing a crinoline under a dress or testing the belts in a car's engine. Both activities worked well some decades ago; today, however, fashions have drastically changed, and car engines are mostly sealed affairs that can only be tinkered with and diagnosed through computer programs. Eschewing split infinitives, once accepted as an inviolable rule, is the same.

29

So, as an accomplished and up-to-date veteran teacher, your list of language prohibitions should center on the contemporary use of language and on the practical realities. But your first rule? *Communicate clearly to your audience.* And, if you can work with your students toward this necessity and how to fulfill this dictate, you are doing your job as a language teacher.

As a teacher, though, you need to be comfortable with this kind of ideal. If you truly believe there is only one correct language (and that includes the components of vocabulary, syntax, and level of formality) that is serviceable in all, or even almost all, situations, if you believe that there is only one audience, you are not going to be open to the suggestions that follow, nor are you likely to equip your students for the world outside of school. If, however, you agree that language is largely context based (and this is where audience comes in) and that facility in a variety of contexts is a mark of an effective language user, *then this section will help you.*

 **WE ALL ENCOUNTER** *language varieties, and depending on the situation, we may experience different reactions to the way we speak. For example, most of the men in my family are firefighters, paramedics, or police officers in New York City. They are incredibly smart, brave, and admirable people—and when they get together with their work buddies, they often speak in working-class vernacular English. They will say, for instance,* he don't know, *where others might say* he doesn't know. *Or they might say* Me and her went to the fire, *not* She and I went to the fire. *Since most of my friends and workmates are English teachers or professors of other subjects, my habit is to speak in standardized English. When I hang out with my family and their workmates, I can stick out like a celery stalk in a basket of buffalo wings.*

When I talk, just about everyone can tell from my usage that I'm not an insider. It's OK because they still treat me well—as well as they treat anyone, at least—and I like their stories. But it's still true that my habitual way of speaking outs me constantly. If that outsider status did cause me problems, I'd have to consider deliberately changing the way I speak when I'm with them (if I could) or deal with the consequences. And, if I ever did something so rude as to tell them that their use of English is wrong (which it isn't), I would deserve the smackdown I'd surely get.

WORKING WITH STUDENTS AND AUDIENCE-RESPONSIVE LANGUAGE

Audience is a crucial issue in communication. As we put it in *CTJ2*, "the audience rules and is also judge, jury, and executioner" (Lindblom and Christenbury 134). What can you ask your students to do to become more aware of communication with an audience, to compose what we call "audience-responsive" communication? You can start with an activity that establishes a narrative and then, depending on audience, varies the factual and emotional components of the communication. With your class, you can work through the following approach:

▸ Establish with your class a **shared narrative** with a set of basic facts and a relatively high-stakes outcome.

▸ Establish with your class a **set of audiences** for this narrative.

▸ Create at least **two different versions** of the narrative that could be effective with two different specified audiences.

▸ **Compare and contrast** the differences of the versions, looking at vocabulary, sentence length, syntax, and other appeals tailored to each audience (in *Continuing the Journey 2*, we discuss this under the topic of *triangulation* [Lindblom and Christenbury 53–56]).

What might you and your students create? Consider the following possibilities.

Narratives

- A *minor car wreck* in which the writer is the driver and there are numerous important details (for instance, weather, speed, confusing traffic signs, possible misbehavior by other drivers) as mitigating circumstances.

- A *missed project deadline* crucial to a semester grade, with multiple problem factors (timeliness of project teammates, personal circumstances, computer and printing glitches, clarity of project content and deadline dates).

- A *snafu in communication* with a close friend resulting in hurt feelings and estrangement (communication issues might involve missed texts, misunderstanding of language, past patterns of communication with this particular friend).

Audiences

- Adult with authority in the situation

- Adult who is sympathetic but who has no authority in the situation

- Peer who is a friend

- Peer who is not a friend

- Parent

- Sibling

- Other relative

- People who follow you on social media (such as Facebook and LinkedIn) and whom you have designated as your audience

- People who follow you on social media and who are part of a general, broader audience (such as Twitter and Instagram)

Possible Alternate Versions

Fact is, most of us tailor our communications to make ourselves more sympathetic, more understandable, more appealing. Some of this can verge on the untruthful, but much of this kind of "curating" of communication is simply human nature and part of successful communication. Accordingly, the teacher or parent who receives the explanation for the project's missed deadline will hear a somewhat altered set of facts from those a sympathetic peer hears. The investigating police officer for the minor car wreck will be offered a differently communicated version than that to a sibling to whom the event is recounted. A valued friend who has been hurt or offended will be given an explanation, with certain selected facts, and that explanation will not be identical to that given to a less-familiar peer. Audience shapes communication, and while our students know this and actually practice it on a daily basis, bringing it into the classroom and highlighting it as part of language instruction is much to our benefit. In fact, in some classrooms where audience-responsive language is not taught, young people learn an unfortunate and inaccurate lesson: that all communication must occur in the same so-called *correct* manner.

EVALUATING NARRATIVES

Be aware that evaluating this kind of communication exercise is the province of the veteran teacher, not necessarily of the novice, especially given cultural mores in some communities. At this point in your career, your hard-earned assurance with your students, your willingness to take risks, and your understanding that the assessment of this activity is indeed subjective position you well to teach language in all its complexity. Because of the multiple variables and the questions regarding effectiveness, there is no ideal rubric for this kind of activity. Your talents as a veteran teacher are therefore vital to being able to design and give valuable and engaging assignments, support and monitor students' work, and then assess student work accurately. What you are looking for, of course, is the creative nuancing of a basic set of facts, all done in the name of more effective communication with a specific audience.

And we know you can do it.

LANGUAGE PLAY AND CELEBRATING THE INVENTIVE

Another aspect of language that is useful to explore with our students is the fact that language morphs and changes, particularly in response to cultural changes and how people actually use language. This inventiveness is part of the strength of English, and one clear example is provided yearly by the American Dialect Society.

THE WORD OF THE YEAR

The American Dialect Society has an annual contest to select the Word of the Year (WOTY), a single word (or phrase) whose currency has become important to the year's discourse. In addition to that single word, other WOTY categories include the subcategories Political, Digital, Slang, Most Useful, Most Likely to Succeed, Least Likely to Succeed, Most Outrageous, Most Euphemistic, Most Unnecessary, and Most Creative. There is even an Emoji of the Year (Pullum).

Interested parties gather and discuss candidates, voting to select a single word of importance. A recent participant observes:

> The very idea of a Word of the Year suggests that words have an existence of
> their own and can do things, like encapsulating a zeitgeist or even influencing
> the tides of human affairs. But I don't think that's right.
>
> What I saw [during the WOTY voting] in the Empire Ballroom was a rapid-
> ly shifting pattern of ethical, aesthetic, and political sentiment that inclined peo-
> ple, apparently in an extraordinarily subjective way, to feel more or less warmth
> toward particular suggested words or phrases. (Pullum)

In 2018 the American Dialect Society's 2017 Word of the Year was, not surprisingly, *fake news*, and runners-up included *alternative facts, #MeToo, pussyhat,* and *take a knee.* The 2016 honorees included *post-truth, woke, gaslight,* and *tweetstorm* (Nilsen; Nilsen and Nilsen).

Once students have been introduced to this idea and event, it is no huge step to have a class choose a WOTY or word of the week or word of the month and post it in the class and discuss it. Language is used to great effect and power in students' social media and personal lives, and they also pick up words and phrases from the adult word. What would your students choose on any given week or month? Ask them, and then spend some time exploring the etymology of the word and the use. Where did they first hear the word? Who uses this word and in what context? What is the relation of this word to adult audiences (i.e., is it something that is often, rarely, or never used outside a peer group?)?

This kind of privileging of student language use may have the effect of reinforcing to students that they too are language creators and language users. *Baeless* and *voluntold* are two such new and inventive words; what else might your students have heard and possibly used?

Former high school English teacher and current professor of English teacher education, Christian Goering has an inventive way to engage students in the nuances of language: writing song lyrics. He's strumming his guitar in our Teachers' Lounge, and luckily he can talk and strum at the same time. Incidentally, if you want to hear Dr. Goering's music chops, check out his album *Big Engine*, which Ken loves. Dr. Goering is also coeditor of the 2018 *Critical Media Literacy and Fake News in Post-Truth America*.

──── FROM THE TEACHERS' LOUNGE ────

Crafting Inventive Language Users through Songwriting

Christian Z. Goering
University of Arkansas, Fayetteville, Arkansas

A full one-third of any given English language arts course pays close attention to the use of language, the other two-thirds focusing on literature and writing. While there are practically as many approaches to teaching language as there are people teaching it, one particular method I've found of creating inventive and skillful students of language

is through song or lyric writing. Giving students the opportunity to create original song lyrics forces them to fit big ideas into small linguistic spaces, the structure inherent in a song lyric. As Nashville singer-songwriter Mary Gauthier shared in a 2015 workshop, "[A] syllable in a song lyric is precious real estate, the most valuable currency in which songwriters deal." After all, there are few syllables in any given song. What I've learned as a songwriter and what I know as an English teacher come together to help students choose language more judiciously and, in the process, create power and precision with their language. Disclaimer: while I advocate for arts-integrated and musically rich approaches to teaching English, a teacher needs zero musical ability to successfully execute this approach.

Before diving into the lyric writing, it's most helpful to determine a topic or source of inspiration. My experiences have taught me that if students have some text to work with, they are more likely to be successful. From a short story or piece of nonfiction to a newspaper article or short video, whatever students choose can often tie directly to other elements of the curriculum (e.g., characters from a novel study). I start by choosing a song lyric with student input, and together we analyze the structure of the lyric. How many verses are there? How many lines per verse? How many syllables per line? Is there a chorus? A bridge? Next, we take a single verse of the song and, breaking into groups of two or three, students start crafting their ideas into the ready-made structure. If possible, I play the music from the borrowed structure through classroom speakers while students are creating their lyrics.

As students dig into lyric writing, they access many of the skills that songwriters use in their craft, ranging from the use of figurative language to action verbs to concrete nouns. Of course, my goals with songwriting extend beyond this introductory activity and do eventually include students creating their own melodies, structures, and unique original songs.

By taking these first steps together with their students, teachers have the potential to harness some of the power necessary in songwriting given the small space to convey often large and complex ideas. While syllables are a currency of songwriting, songs themselves are a currency of adolescence. By having students write original lyrics, you help them develop the tools to tell their stories while also building skills valued by English teachers everywhere.

MISSES AND NEAR MISSES IN LANGUAGE

Language can be used and misused in many contexts. One instance Leila sees a great deal is the mild but persistent misuse of the phrase "reign them in" (the king or queen decrees?) when, referencing a time when horses were far more common as transportation, the correct phrase is "rein them in" (whoa, Nellie). You too hear and know about a number of these kinds of misses and near misses, and some of them, along with their humor, can tell us a great deal about language use, about what we hear and assume (as in the case of "reign/rein"), and, further, about how history changes the pertinence of many of our familiar phrases. Another phrase of interest is the frequent use among young people of "based off" in place of "based on," as in, "The film was based off the book of the same name." Oddly enough, in this context, the words *on* and *off*, usually antonyms, act as synonyms. In 2014, Grammar Girl said this use was likely to increase, even though it's logically incorrect (Fogarty). In our experience, its use has indeed increased.

THE PURSUIT OF *correctness can have wholly unexpected results, and one case in point is a little self-published book that an elderly and long-retired colleague of mine put together for her students, friends, and community. She presented the book to me some years ago with the*

expressed and heartfelt hope that I would find it useful. I read it soon after and have kept it ever since—and while I have not used it as she wished, it is a terrific example of unintended consequences.

My colleague's book is arranged alphabetically with the expressed and wholly admirable intention of providing "just the right word from A–Z." It features, however, not words but phrases, some of which are produced in the following, taken word for word from this unintentionally fractured gem of a language handbook:

> *"Our company could never communicate without drawing blood."*
>
> *"After the committee threw out chains of logic, we breathed a sign of relief."*
>
> *"Are you aware of the victimizing cesspool where children are abused?"*
>
> *"You're a man who looks like an owl after he's made a jackass out of himself."*

And the following, which depend on mishearing of common phrases (see roman text*):*

> *Jim Smolder runs* for and aft.
>
> *Let's try to eliminate the* legal limbo.
>
> *We were certainly at* mute-point *when we learned of Josephine's illness.*

Beyond the chuckle this book still gives me, it is also useful in many ways. Having students look at these kinds of mixed and misinterpreted phrases can be not only engaging but also instructive; what about these aphorisms (and students can contribute some themselves) can be changed, corrected, or rewritten? How is it that these specific mistakes are made?

Students can have an instructive time looking at *limbo/lingo*, *moot/mute*, etc. and create some of these themselves. The technical term, *malapropism* (most widely known through the satire in Richard Sheridan's eighteenth-century play "The Rivals"), may not be intriguing to students, but presented as "just the right word," students may be far more interested in exploring these miscommunications.

A RENEWED LANGUAGE CHALLENGE: MORE COMPLETE GENDER AWARENESS

The acceptability of using *he* as the one standard singular pronoun has changed in English, and we read few writers and hear few speakers who use a "universal" male pronoun. Our beloved language, however, doesn't help us a great deal when the singular is meant to indicate two or more genders, and for some speakers this can lead to asserting that "the rules" will not allow them to mix the number (*every student should take their book* vs. *every student should take his or her book*).

Noted American language expert Bryan Garner, in the latest version of his usage manual, suggests singular *they* as a sensible resolution to this issue:

> Speakers of AmE [American English] resist this development more than speakers of BrE [British English], in which the indeterminate *they* is already more or less standard. That it sets many literate Americans' teeth on edge is an unfortunate obstacle to what promises to be the ultimate solution to the problem. (4th ed. 822)

Garner's 2009 edition has this same passage verbatim.

Our professional organization NCTE also offers some guidelines here—newly revised in 2018—mostly common sense and also underscored by the authority of two highly respected style manuals. NCTE's guidelines also result from a new understanding of transgender people and their frequent exclusion in standardized English Language. The *Statement on Gender and Language* opens language to the knowledge that gender (a social construction created by society and imposed on individuals) is different from biological sex, which is often assigned at birth based on external bodily features. Some agender and transgender people prefer to go by *they*, and some may go by *he* or by *she.* You may notice that more and more people list their desired pronouns on their email signatures and social media profiles. NCTE's newest statement acknowledges this situation, inviting both teachers and students to use pronouns that are inclusive. (For more on transgender issues in education, see Miller.) The statement is specific:

- Avoid using *he* as a universal pronoun; likewise, avoid using binary alternatives such as *he/she, he or she,* or *(s)he.*

- As the editors of the recent editions of the *Chicago Manual of Style* (2017), the *Associated Press Stylebook* (2018), and other style guides affirm, the pronoun *they* is appropriate to use in writing when referring to singular antecedents, including when writing for publication.

- Unless the gender of a singular personal antecedent is otherwise specified, use the gender-neutral singular pronouns *they, them, their,* and *theirs.*

- The *Chicago Manual of Style* affirms that the pronoun *themself* may be used to signal a singular antecedent; that some people may alternatively prefer to use *themselves* to signal a singular antecedent; and that a person's stated preference should be respected.

- *Are* is the present-tense verb for the singular pronoun *they,* just as *are* is the present-tense verb for the singular pronoun *you.*

- When referring to any individual, respect that individual's chosen pronoun usage, or lack thereof. (Note: while the singular *they* is the most common nonbinary pronoun, there are others, including but not limited to *ey/em/eirs* and *ze/hir/hirs.*)

NCTE also offers some specifics regarding usage, which may help clarify the points made above:

Exclusionary (binary):

Every cast member should know **his or her** lines by Friday.

Inclusive (any gender):

Each cast member should know **their** lines by Friday.

Inclusive (student whose chosen pronouns are *they/them/theirs*):

Alex needs to learn **their** lines by Friday.

Exclusionary (binary):

Each should wait until **he/she** is notified of **his/her** test results.

Inclusive (any gender):

Each should wait until **they** are notified of their test results.

Inclusive (student whose chosen pronouns are *they/them/theirs*):

Janani should wait until **they** are notified of **their** test results.

(*Statement on Gender and Language*)

NCTE emphasizes the need for the responsible use of language regarding students and their gender identities because all should "feel visible, heard, valued, and protected." NCTE affirms that "[a] student's pronouns intersect profoundly with their gender identity and their sense of self." Practical guidelines include:

▸ Give each student a private way to let you know their name and chosen pronouns. . . .

▸ Respect each student's chosen name and pronouns.

▸ Respect a student's privacy and keep a student's communication about gender identity confidential. A transgender student may or may not feel comfortable or safe having their gender identity known in all contexts, and therefore may not use the same pronouns in all contexts, even within one school. Maintain confidentiality, attention, and discretion in communicating with and about the student, and do not disclose any student's gender identity in any setting without the student's clear consent.

▸ Because, like other elements of identity, a student's gender identity may be fluid rather than static, remain attuned to and supportive of possible shifts in a student's chosen name and pronouns; again, maintain confidentiality and do not disclose any shift in a student's gender identity without the student's consent.

As noted in a previous chapter, how we are named is an important issue, and for both teachers and students it is vital that we go by the name we freely choose. This is one of the most important aspects of language use, and one of the most powerful. We do acknowledge that for some in our society acceptance of transgender individuals and how they wish to be addressed is not a resolved issue; for us as conscientious teachers, however, it seems vital that we use language with our students that respects and embraces, and that does not divide or alienate.

A RECURRING LANGUAGE CHALLENGE: RACIALLY CHARGED AND RACIST WORDS

The power of language is one of the most potent arguments English teachers make about why our subject matter counts. Wars, treaties, friendships, love relationships are all affected by the words we use and the language in which we couch our wishes and desires. In an increasingly connected society, however, the public use of some words remains extraordinarily contentious, even to the extent that the use of certain words by certain groups can be seen as socially and morally repugnant. *Racially charged* is one way we can describe these words (examples might be *tribal, urban, disadvantaged*). For other words and terms, however, the term *racist* more often than not applies, and when we—especially if we are majority race teachers—use such words (any racial slur, including the *n*-word), the possibilities for hurt, misunderstanding, and anger abound. This is true even when we are quoting from a text or another person.

Perhaps the most powerful and also most infamous example of a racist term is the *n*-word. When it is used, in particular by White speakers in a school context, we enter very rocky terrain. This is an issue when we as secondary English teachers use classical literature such as *Adventures of Huckleberry Finn, To Kill a Mockingbird, Native Son, Black Boy*, and even a number of YA novels (examples include the Mildred Taylor series, including *Roll of Thunder, Hear My Cry; The Absolutely True Diary of a Part-Time Indian* by Sherman Alexie; and *The Hate U Give* by Angie Thomas). The historical, cultural, and artistic aspects of these titles, however, can aid readers of all races, and often—not always, but often—these considerations can mitigate concerns about the contextual use of toxic and incendiary racial slurs. It is worth noting that *English Journal* addressed this issue a few years ago in a focus issue devoted to the controversy of teaching *Adventures of Huckleberry Finn*; see Connors and Thomas if you would like to read the varying points of view and the teaching approaches. It is also worth noting that any cursory search of the banned books list of the American Library Association (ALA), as well as of news articles, will confirm that parents, communities, and students often challenge the use of literature that contains racially charged or racist terms, even when those terms are used in a historical context.

In two nationally prominent recent cases, however, it is university-level students who have been in the news, registering shock and objection to *any* use of the *n*-word for any reason and in any context. In early 2019, for instance, a university history professor allowed a student in his honors class to read a quotation that featured the *n*-word, and the professor later led a discussion about the racial slur using, in that discussion, the *n*-word itself. The incident did not go well. As reported in news articles, for the class as a whole, it did not matter that the quotation came from the work they were studying, James Baldwin's *The Fire Next Time*; it did not matter that a peer had read the quotation in context; and it did not matter that the professor was subsequently asking about Baldwin's assertions, all of which centered on the power of the racial slur. Students objected, they questioned the professor's judgment, and administrators listened. The university's response was to suspend the professor and remove him from teaching and program duties (Osei).

In a second recent incident in spring 2019, also at the university level, a law professor at the University of Chicago used the *n*-word as an apt illustration of the "'fighting words' doctrine . . . the use of language that could incite violence" (Bartlett). Because of student objections, again, regardless of the context, the professor concluded that "I'm persuaded that the value [of using the word and the illustration] is offset by the distraction and harm it causes," and while his teaching of the "fighting words" doctrine continues, he will not be using the *n*-word in class again (Bartlett). Somewhat ironically, the professor is well known in the free speech community and is coeditor of a recent book, *The Free Speech Century.*

For us at the secondary level, these two cases are of real import and illustrate, certainly, the kind of sensitivity we must exercise in our classes with our younger students. Literature can provide context, but when we talk about such loaded words within language lessons—and there may be, at this time in history, no more loaded word than the *n*-word—we would do well to proceed with caution. Our intentions can be misconstrued, and students of all races can leave our classroom with more injury and pain than just a wrong impression.

But please don't take this as a sign that we suggest ELA teachers of any race cower from the study of the controversies of language. Far from it. We highly recommend raising these issues boldly, intelligently, and sensitively. When Ken was editor of *English Journal,* he published a 2011 issue titled "Beyond Grammar: The Richness of English Language" that included articles on teaching vocabulary, shifts in grammar instruction, language play, and studying multiple translations of a literary work. One of the most remarkable articles was "Dangerous Words: Recognizing the Power of Language by Researching Derogatory Terms" by Karen A. Keely. In it Keely describes how her students engaged in an in-depth study of the origins and development of racist, misogynist, ableist, and other discriminatory terms. Keely sought support from her school administrators before teaching the unit, which, according to her fascinating article, went into unprecedented territory and fared quite well. The kind of courage, commitment, and competence Keely shows is what we should demand of ourselves as veteran English teachers.

SPELLING AND LANGUAGE

There is a general concern about spelling and the Wild West that spelling may be turning into, especially with the wide use of the internet and other social media platforms that encourage inventive words and abbreviations (*r* for *are*; *u* for *you; NSFW* for "not safe for work"; *PIR* for "parent in room"). One British linguistic expert, David Crystal, cautions, however, that while "[p]rophets of doom have suggested that, because the Internet motivates so much spelling variation . . . a standard English spelling system has no future. They are wrong" (270–71). He elaborates:

> We mustn't exaggerate the problem. If [the spelling of] nearly a quarter of the words in English are variable, this means that over three-quarters are not. And most of the common words in the language display no variation at all. Standard spelling is a reality. The vast majority of the words I read in an American newspaper are spelled in exactly the same way as their equivalents in . . . English-language newspapers, magazines, books, and website and printed ephemera all over the world. . . . A standard spelling system will continue to be important, but the range of alternatives that are accepted as standard will change. (221, 275)

What does this advice mean for us as teachers? Crystal advises that we teach words in realistic contexts and with other related words (279) and that we stop giving students lists of spelling words, which is a method that not only defies "all the basic principles of language acquisition" (280), but it just doesn't work. Positive suggestions include:

- Associating the correct spelling with the realistic context (The *principal* enforced the *principle*)

- Using word families, groups of words sharing the same root (*sign, signs, signing, signal, signaling*)

- Reminding students that their pronunciation will often not match the spelling of the word (*libry, litrature, pome, reconized*)

- Making word lists with words that students might actually use in writing (Crystal 280–85, 289)

It bears repeating that language morphs and changes. And there have been concerted efforts to change spelling conventions. Around the turn from the nineteenth to the twentieth century in the United States, a group called the Simple Spelling Society formed, and included powerful people such as Andrew Carnegie, Thomas Dewey, Mark Twain, William

James, and President Theodore Roosevelt. Their goal was to make spelling more logical and easier, spelling, for example, *bred* instead of *bread* and *paragraf* instead of *paragraph* (Dunn and Lindblom 52). They failed, of course, demonstrating that spelling is more a matter of habit or tradition than planning and logic.

It's also possible to go way overboard with spelling, and there is a history in the United States of doing exactly that. For example, in the mid-nineteenth to early twentieth century at Illinois State Normal University, one of the first major teachers colleges in the Midwest, students were expected to get 100 percent right on twenty-five-word spelling tests every day throughout an entire course. If they ever misspelled (or even corrected a misspelling) in their future classes, they had to take the course again. Poor spelling was considered "evil," and it was every student's moral responsibility to rid themselves of this demon (Lindblom, Banks, and Quay). Grammar and spelling skills continue to be connected arbitrarily to moral goodness to this day (Dunn and Lindblom), and we suggest teachers examine their own practices to see if this overzealousness regarding surface issues exists in their own teaching. Spelling errors are easy to detect and correct; ask yourself honestly, do you spend more time on this issue than on the more difficult and higher-level issues of effective communication?

LANGUAGE NUANCE AND SENTENCE COMBINING

As a veteran teacher, you are most likely well familiar with sentence combining, in which short sentence "stems" can be used to make a longer, more syntactically complex sentence. These practices have been shown to encourage genuine improvement in student writing. Working with short stems and longer sentences can help students who are stuck on subject-verb-object patterns in their writing, and it shows them, through imitation and practice, how they can vary their work, lengthen their sentences, and create prose that is more complex. While what we suggest below should not be used with students in long class sessions— it can be wearying to look at these kinds of nuances and to talk about them for big blocks of time—in short bursts, this variation on sentence combining can help students more surely attune themselves to the nuances of language.

Thus the bare facts, in this case four short sentences,

I studied hard for the test.

It took two grueling hours to take.

I was disappointed.

I did not pass.

can become

Though I studied hard for the test, and it took two grueling hours to take, I was disappointed I did not pass.

or

I was disappointed that I did not pass the test even though I studied hard for it and it took two grueling hours to take.

or

I did not pass—and I was disappointed—the grueling two-hour test, for which I studied hard.

or

I studied hard for the two-hour test; I was disappointed because I did not pass.

Beyond the benefits of combining short stems into longer pieces of discourse, any combined stems result in sentences that often imply somewhat different things and have different emphases. For instance, looking at the possible four variations, note the differences in punctuation and the placement of the four facts:

A. *Though I studied hard for the test, and it took two grueling hours to take, I was disappointed that I did not pass.*

B. *I was disappointed that I did not pass the test even though I studied hard for it and it took two grueling hours to take.*

C. *I did not pass—and I was disappointed—the grueling two-hour test, for which I studied hard.*

D. *I studied hard for the two-hour test; I was disappointed because I did not pass.*

In an open classroom conversation, with the possible variants of the sentences clearly projected so that everyone can see them, students can consider and debate the relative emphases of these four versions. In small groups, they may query, for instance:

- Which of the four emphasizes the importance of having studied and spent two hours of testing? (Answer: possibly both A and B)

- Which emphasizes most emphatically the point that I did not pass? (Answer: most likely C)

- Which emphasizes most emphatically the disappointment? (Answer: again, most likely C)

- Which seems to pay more attention to not passing? (Answer: a good candidate is D)

- What is the difference in the emotion conveyed in the two sentences that, respectively, use dashes (C) and a semicolon (D)? (Answer: it could be argued that the dashes in C are far more emphatic and therefore emotional than the rather restrained semicolon in D)

- What happens to the importance of the length of the test when *two-hour* becomes an adverb (C and D) as opposed to part of a phrase (A and B)? (Answer: making *two-hour* an adverb tucks it neatly into the test itself; having the length of the test part of a separate phrase makes it more important)

Creation of useful stems can come from students, from literature (breaking long sentences into stems and then recombining them; see Deborah Dean's "Shifting Perspectives in Grammar: Changing What and How We Teach" for some excellent examples taken from YA literature), or from sentence combining workbooks. Combining the stems can be "open," as above, or "signaled" (most sentence combining books give explicit directions regarding which signal to use when). The overall point, however, is not what is done with the final combined sentences, not if any or all of them are "correct" or complete, but what the different versions convey.

For veteran teachers who are comfortable with open exploratory conversations—not every student will agree with the characterizations of created sentences—and are confident of their own linguistic abilities, using sentence combining to explore language nuances can be a highly productive ten minutes of class. In limited doses, this kind of activity can point students to language differences and encourage them to examine syntactic structures (such as introductory phrases) and punctuation (such as dashes and semicolons) with a far keener eye than they might have before. This side benefit asks students to look at usage, punctuation, and syntactical terms—and if you want to discuss these sentences and their differences, you will need to use and know terms such as *adverb, subject/noun, verb,* etc.

BUT KORRECTNESS HAS IT'S PLACE—DON'T IT?

Although it is appropriate and important for our students to know about the nuances of language, have an awareness of language change, and acknowledge the differences in audiences, as well as be sensitive to issues of gender and race, we must also acknowledge that paying close attention to traditional forms of correctness is truly important. If we leave students with the mistaken idea that any language goes any time, we are not doing our job. In final draft work, in anything related to job interviews or work, in formal communications, our students need to pay appropriate attention to spelling, pronunciation, and traditional usage and grammatical forms. We must be careful, in this wonderful and intellectual and rich discussion, to make distinctions about degrees of language issues and correctness, and we can offer guidance and cautions.

Look, for instance, at the head for this section, "But Korrectness Has It's Place—Don't It?" The prohibition against starting a sentence with a conjunction, in this case *but,* is another fake rule. In highly formal writing, this practice is discouraged, but it is not by any means wrong or an error. Using conjunctions (*but* as well as *and, or, nor*) to begin sentences is a **stylistic choice** that can, in many instances, be highly effective. In this case, the *but* signals that a previous argument or discussion has already occurred (and, indirectly, in this chapter, it has), and the *but* gives the reader an indication that now the topic will be addressed. Which, now, it is.

Another issue is the second word, *Korrectness*, in this section's head. *Korrectness* for *correctness* is nonstandard, for sure, but it is also lively, even a bit trendy, and we all see similar spellings in social media and in advertising for trade names. Such **playful respellings**, especially using *k* for *c* (think, in advertising and product names, of *krazy, kleen, kwuik, kool, kut, skool*), are often clear attempts to attract a consumer's attention (Crystal 225 ff.) with a tinge of resistance or protest and can be seen in such variants as *Kut Hut, Krazy Glue, Kozi Korner*, etc. These kinds of language forms are not necessarily in the category of "incorrect" and are instead variants, considering the context, that can seem knowing and sophisticated.

A third issue to consider when we look at "But Korrectness Has It's Place—Don't It?" is the confusion between *its* and *it's*, both an ongoing and a losing battle of sorts, and also what we might term a **low-level error**. We English teachers may be some of the last speakers of the language to insist that the singular neuter possessive, *its*, unlike every other possessive, doesn't sport an apostrophe (yes, this may seem illogical, as *his* and *hers* are also single possessives without apostrophes, but who sees *hi's* or *her's*?). While some predict that the distinction between *its* (possessive) and *it's* (contraction for *it is*) will eventually fade, leaving *it's* to win the field for both instances, attacking this kind of usage error is misguided because it falls more in the territory of faux pas, an error for which there is little real consequence. Yes, it may seem great to us, but its not fatal regarding it's use (hope you see what we did there).

But consider the fourth issue of the head "But Korrectness Has It's Place—Don't It?" For some, the last two words are tantamount to linguistic mortal sins and/or felonies. These kinds of errors, in this case a mismatch between subject (*Korrectness*) and verb (*don't*, which should be *doesn't*), are **stigmatized forms** and are errors that are disproportionately—and unfairly— tied to speaker intelligence, education, and social standing. Thus, the "tax" on routinely saying *don't it* or *he don't* or *me and her was*, for instance, can be very high, and we need to reinforce with students that while these kinds of forms may well be used without concern in informal speech, in their own homes, and in all sorts of relaxed social situations, they may have significant consequences in other contexts, as we discuss more fully in Chapter 2.

On a positive note, we English teachers realize that enhanced **reading and hearing** foster correctness; when students are exposed in our classrooms to language that adheres to standard forms, the chances of their replicating the same are enhanced (correct spelling is also positively affected). Truth be told, we are playing the long game, the benefits of which may not be readily apparent in our classrooms. Consistent reading and hearing may not change every student's daily speaking, writing, and spelling patterns on a significant level, but when students know and have enforced that certain audiences will indeed expect correctness—and make assumptions when it is not present—we are doing our jobs as language teachers.

CONCLUSION

Language, like so much of the content in English language arts, is an ocean. The surface of the water may be smooth, but the depths harbor shoals, caves, and treasures. Our students, language users and language makers, can both learn in our classrooms and bring to us and their peers their own rich experience with language. Tapping into their expertise—and offering them ours—makes for a generative and mutually beneficial language experience and opens the world of effective and inventive language use. We can't really claim expertise about exactly what kinds of language students will be required to master, but we can equip them with the knowledge, attitudes, and determination that will help them continue to grow on their own journeys as effective communicators.

Today's Challenges for Speaking

Technology, particularly the prevalence of smartphone screens, has encouraged young people to become at ease, even extraordinarily comfortable, with writing. Direct messages, texts, Snapchat and Instagram, blogs, and other forms of social media have resulted in young people who write—actually form written words and sentences in informal conversation—far more often and more fluidly than have young people in previous generations. In fact, today many young people prefer written texts to phone calls, and this includes not just to adults but also to their closest friends. Stranger still, at least to some of us oldsters, is that some young people, even when they are in a room together, occasionally prefer to text each other rather than speak to each other. To complicate this new order, they sometimes do both simultaneously.

Virtually any meal involving young people who are allowed to have phones at the table results in a multifaceted conversation. There's an over-the-table conversation going on in which all are involved. But under the table (literally), there's another conversation going on via cell phones. The adults may or may not be aware of this back-channel conversation, but it is happening. Given the young people in Ken's life, he assumes it's better if he doesn't know the contents of those conversations.

Young people's preferences for and experience with writing have probably had some benefit on students' ability and willingness to compose in writing. But how about their speaking? If young people use writing so easily through technology, does it make sense that there would be a corresponding downturn in young people's ability and willingness to speak? Some educators and social critics have become concerned that this is the case. Alarmed that "conversational competence might be the single most overlooked skill we fail to teach students," educator Paul Barnwell raises the issue in *The Atlantic*.

When students apply for colleges and jobs, they won't conduct interviews through their smart phones. When they negotiate pay raises and discuss projects with employers, they should exude a thoughtful presence and demonstrate the ability to think on their feet (or at least without Google). When they face significant life decisions, they must be able to think things through and converse with their partners. If the majority of their conversations are based on fragments pin-balled back and forth through a screen, how will they develop the ability to truly communicate in person? (n.p.)

Virginia teacher Peter S. Willis agrees with Barnwell's position, and he's been working with his students to offset what he sees as their decreasing speaking and listening skills. Mr. Willis is in our Teachers' Lounge to tell us more.

—— FROM THE TEACHERS' LOUNGE ——

Using Book Talks to Get Students Speaking in Class

Peter S. Willis
Manchester High School, Chesterfield, Virginia

When I began my teaching career, it seemed that my students couldn't stop talking to each other. But as the years have passed—and smartphones and social media have come to monopolize more and more of my students' attention—I have witnessed a steady decline in their speaking  *and listening skills. They simply don't seem to invest time in face-to-face interaction, which is the most essential task involved in learning how to interact with others. Consequently, when students arrive in my senior*

English classes, they often bring incomplete speaking and listening skills that manifest through their discomfort during group activities.

To encourage my students to interact more with their peers and me, I conduct book talks based on fiction and nonfiction independent reading time that takes place in the first twenty minutes of class. For a few days each month, my students and I put away laptops and smartphones and come together informally to share thoughts and reflections about the books that we have read during our independent reading time. For the first few book talks, I serve as the first speaker and share my thoughts and reflections about the book or books I have been reading, to model for my students how to speak in an informal setting. We have no set structure for the book talks, though I expect my students to speak with specificity about the characters, plots, and settings of their books for fiction works or about the ideas, events, and people for nonfiction works. To build listening skills, I encourage students to respond to speakers with questions and observations of their own. As the year progresses and students become acclimated to the format, our book talks become more engaging and expressive as speakers present the merits or faults of a particular text or author, and audience members question or challenge a speaker's views.

Even though I emphasize a relaxed approach to the book talks, some students balk at sharing their thoughts and observations with their peers. They feel uncomfortable speaking in front of others, even among friends and classmates they have known for years. Therefore, I never force my students to participate when doing so would cause them distress; instead, I meet individually before or after school or during lunches with students who do not feel comfortable or capable of speaking in front of others. Students who have been reluctant to share their thoughts in the classroom often open up during our one-on-one talks and share their ideas more easily and comfortably when their audience is only me. Such

> *talks also give me a chance to develop relationships with reserved students*
> *who might not be comfortable engaging with me in the classroom.*

Speaking skills are important in the workplace as well, of course. A 2018 survey of business executives and hiring managers listed "able to effectively communicate orally" as the highest learning priority among this group and cut across majors (Association of American Colleges & Universities). In tacit agreement, many colleges—including Ken's home institution—have recently added speaking requirements to the core curriculum, a sign that speaking remains an important skill for success. At the K–12 level, many state curriculum lists of critical twenty-first-century skills include oral communication, including working in teams of diverse (even globally diverse) members.

To aid teachers in their instruction, there are some good older texts out there for high school and middle school classrooms, such as Thomas M. McCann et. al.'s *Talking in Class: Using Discussion to Enhance Teaching and Learning*; Barry Gilmore's *Speaking Volumes: How to Get Students Discussing Books—and Much More*; and Nancy Steineke's *Assessment Live! 10 Real-Time Ways for Kids to Show What They Know—and Meet the Standards*. And yet, compared to what's available to assist teachers in writing and reading instruction, there's not much for teachers who wish to emphasize speaking in their classrooms.

THE PROBLEM OF SPEAKING: EVERYWHERE AND NOWHERE

Learning to speak effectively is a skill with ancient roots, its most famous Western proponent probably being Quintilian, the Roman teacher who claimed that the most talented rhetorician would be "the good person speaking well." Quintilian's goal was for ethically good people to be effective enough speakers to motivate and lead those around them. This is a lofty goal, one that is relevant today. Indeed, good parents work hard to ensure that their babies learn to speak by continuously speaking to them, reinforcing when their babies speak back, and pointing out the names of everything around them to increase their babies' oral vocabulary. As children grow, most parents continue this pattern and help their offspring with pronunciation, vocabulary, and even the use and appropriate context for certain phrases and words. When we look at school, however, where is speaking in the ELA curriculum?

How often have you worked with students on the features of oral discourse listed in the previous paragraph? And yet the management of those features of oral communication may be among the most important tasks of any person on any day. In fact, that is part of the problem. Oral communication is everywhere. As a result of its ubiquity, we often forget about it. Speaking becomes a tacit skill that simply exists as a foundation upon which we build everything else. A tale by David Foster Wallace helps illustrate the point:

> There are these two young fish swimming along and they happen to meet an older fish swimming the other way, who nods at them and says "Morning, boys. How's the water?" And the two young fish swim on for a bit, and then eventually one of them looks over at the other and goes "What the hell is water?" (3–4)

We can be so immersed in oral communication that, like fish in water, we forget it's there. So common is the experience of speaking, people even attribute it to inanimate objects when they say things such as "That painting speaks to me." *Speak* has become shorthand for any communication one experiences. But, when we make *speaking* stand for everything, it ends up standing for nothing on its own. Therefore, it takes effort to ensure that speaking is a significant element in an ELA classroom, an end in itself as well as a means for learning other things.

Many teachers include oral reports among their requirements, and especially committed teachers work with students to ensure that their public speaking skills improve. One practical way they do this is by requiring students' peers to evaluate their effectiveness and discuss what the components of effective oral communication are. And there is so much more. Speaking is at the root of most communication, and it entails many features, such as:

- Volume

- Pitch

- Projection

- ▸ Articulation and pronunciation

- ▸ Eye contact

- ▸ Body language

- ▸ Word choice and register

- ▸ Silence, or pauses (the oral equivalent of white space in writing)

- ▸ Facial expression

- ▸ Emphasis

- ▸ Speed, or pace

- ▸ Sentence length, and the use of breath

- ▸ Repetition

- ▸ Rhythm

Like so many elements of the ELA curriculum, speaking is something that seems simple on the surface but is in truth a complex set of abilities. And we haven't yet even discussed how critical thinking is developed by talking. (The widely quoted aphorism "How do I know what I think until I hear what I say?" is pertinent here.) In her *Building Bigger Ideas: A Process for Teaching Purposeful Talk*, Maria Nichols points out that even among very young children, speaking can be an important part of thinking. Effective teachers know this and use speaking activities to unlock students' critical skills:

> A smirk or furrowed brow, a glint in an eye, or a sly smile may hint at what's simmering in a child's mind. For these children, ideas may emerge slowly in turn and talks as they use their partners to help tease out their thinking. Or, their voices may enter a whole-group conversation over time as the collective thinking gradually helps them to strengthen their own. (57)

Oral communication remains an essential skill for all, and it is a skill that can help to develop and unlock other skills and abilities. Clearly, it's a part of the ELA curriculum that deserves as much consideration as reading and writing.

SKILLS OF SPEAKING, SKILLS OF TALKING

Speaking occurs in many different places and in many different forms and for many different purposes. An effective communicator is aware of this and is mindful of their reasons for talking. People talk to communicate information, of course, but talk does much more than that. Speaking also makes an impression on other people, creates and builds relationships both personal and professional, changes or reinforces opinions, relates facts and information, calls for attention, lulls to sleep, entertains, honors, accuses, wounds, comforts, and much more. Oral communication is so positively thick with meaning, including facial expressions and body language, that written communication is not always a good substitute. Note how emojis are now ubiquitous in some forms of informal writing because they add the facial expressions that the printed word alone cannot convey.

Speak and *talk* are pretty much interchangeable; however, for the purposes of instruction, it's useful to separate the terms. Generally, *speaking* refers to situations in which one person is delivering what we might technically call a "discourse." This can be a formal presentation, a monologue or soliloquy, or any other situation in which one person holds the floor for a specific period of time. *Talking*, in contrast, is generally considered the action that occurs in conversation among two or more people. These are not hard-and-fast rules—after all, who among us doesn't occasionally talk to themselves?—but they point to various forms of oral discourse that successful people would want to master.

STRATEGIES OF SPEAKING

▸ **Working from an Outline**

This doesn't mean composing an outline, but rather exhibiting the ability to work *from* an outline, to speak from notes rather than from a script. Doing this requires knowledge of the material and the ability to compose key words that will effectively remind a speaker of all they have to say.

> **Combating Nervousness**

We all get nervous in different ways. Ken is fond of saying that when he is nervous, he gets *bigger;* that is, he talks faster and more loudly, and he gets more outlandishly jokey than usual. When he is comfortable, he settles down and can appear more poised. Some others get *smaller* when they are nervous. Their volume decreases, they hide behind a podium, and they look in a downward direction. It helps students to diagnose their own reaction to nervousness and understand their behaviors. This will be enormously informative as they practice in front of a mirror (or better yet, a camera) to try to get past their jitters. Ultimately, though, the only thing that really helps students with serious, even paralyzing apprehension—we think of stage fright—is practice and appropriately scaffolded experience. What do we recommend? Three strategies may help:

> Let especially nervous students speak for a shorter time, more frequently.

> Let them begin by reading from a script before moving to notes or key words.

> Have them present in front of the class in groups before being expected to present alone.

Our goal as veteran teachers should be for all students to be able to comfortably present to an audience of strangers. A staff writer from *The Atlantic* wrote an interesting piece on students who are using social media to protest requirements that they deliver formal presentations in front of live audiences (Lorenz). Their reasons are primarily that, for some especially anxious students, presenting before a live audience might be too traumatic, and they prefer other options, such as presenting privately to the teacher or writing an essay.

With all due respect to these students and the educators who support them, we disagree. It's not appropriate for us to allow students to opt out of learning important skills.

Instead, we must scaffold and support students as they take on increasingly more complex and difficult tasks. Veteran teachers can do this in a caring and supportive way, getting help and advice from colleagues, parents, and the students themselves. That *Atlantic* article, however, could be excellent fodder for a lively class discussion!

▸ **Speaking/Responding to a Specific Audience**

No audience is just like any other audience. We teachers know this in our guts because of the many times we've taught the same lesson on the same day to two groups of students at the same level in the same building—and had the class and its outcomes be completely different. Each audience has its own chemistry and it reacts differently to the same stimuli. Good speakers sense the needs of their audience as they are speaking. They look for clues in the facial expressions and body language of members of the audience. They even look for the most supportive or most skeptical audience members so they can get some of the energy back that they need to continue to improve their presentation as they deliver it. In a live presentation, the communication really is two-way.

Speaking of being mindful of audience, Molly Potas, a Wyoming teacher who's just stopped into our Teachers' Lounge, has some important advice about equipping students with rhetorical strategies for the many speaking situations they will encounter in their lives.

—— FROM THE TEACHERS' LOUNGE ——

Empowering Students: For the Love of Rhetoric

Molly S. Potas
Meeteetse Schools, Meeteetse, Wyoming

The moment a baby is born, it is gifted the tools of rhetoric. A baby learns quickly that certain squeaks and cries elicit prompt delivery of food, cuddles, relief, or any other desires they want met, sometimes while a parent stands by scrambling and confused as to the specific demand. As children grow older, they automatically fine-tune their rhetorical skills to match their rhetorical situation. It's fascinating to observe a younger child use persuasion

effortlessly on an unassuming parent, friend, or teacher. Let's define this moment a bit more closely.

Here, a kiddo, let's call him Jake, wants to have a sleepover at his friend's house, yet his parents are hesitant. Jake knows beforehand which rhetorical tools he needs in order to persuade his mother into saying yes. Therefore, Jake cleans his room, compliments Mom, and using his best pathos, throwing in an extra "I love you, Mom." Jake knows from previous rhetorical experiences what elevates his chances of Mom saying yes to his request. Dad's easier. Jake heads out to the shop or garage with a sandwich, or something Mom just baked, asserts his simple question to Dad; Dad gives the nod of approval and says to go ask Mom. Jake just completed the rhetorical cycle, because when Jake asks Mom, he even has a yes from Dad, which of course helps his cause. In short, Jake clearly knows certain rhetorical tools work with Mom, yet different rhetorical tools work with Dad, and Jake makes these adjustments without a second's thought. To extend this analogy even further, Jake clearly understands that the rhetorical tools he needs to persuade his brother of something are much different from the devices he must use with a friend. What an exhausting process moving through the various rhetorical situations we face hour by hour each day, yet are we truly tired and fatigued by these rhetorical shifts? I think not.

For the last eighteen years teaching grades 7–12 English, as well as college-level courses, the mighty question emerges for me: How can I teach students, beginning at the formative years, to learn and master specific rhetorical devices in their various speaking activities? Let's ponder this question for a minute. Even though students effortlessly know how to shift through various rhetorical situations in their personal lives, some students can't imagine how to apply such tools to their academic and professional affairs. As educators, it's imperative that we teach students to recognize viable rhetorical situations within academia, which in turn will better prepare students with the necessary skills to flourish in the realms of job and scholarship interviews, professional and technical presentation tasks, college, workforce, military, trades and training, marketing, and more.

Each of us is rhetorically stimulated on a minute-by-minute basis through advertisements, social media, cell phones, our friends, peers, children, and students. Yet I must ask, are we giving our students adequate tools to take charge of, recognize, and assert themselves in purposeful speaking situations by using the classic ethos, logos, and pathos to persuade their specific audiences? Giving students real tools builds confidence and furthers their success by simple instruction and highlighting one of the most valuable skills they have already mastered informally. Using rhetoric as a communicative tool not only in their personal lives but also as a superpower in academic institutions and professional careers gives students more leverage and mindful control in navigating academic and professional learning communities through purposeful speaking.

Molly Potas's ideas have very practical value for the classroom. In that spirit, let's return to more strategies for speaking:

▶ **Developing Stage Presence/Charisma**

It's hard to know what makes someone have stage presence, but we know it when we see someone with it. Have you ever seen a professional actor immediately command attention the moment they walk on stage? We're not all capable of winning acting awards, but we can all learn to develop our own sense of stage presence. Watching gifted speakers and identifying teachers and students in your school who have such presence can offer great clues about what works. Show videos of charismatic speakers and actors and work with your students to identify the skills and behaviors they exhibit. Take these ideas seriously with your students in conversation, and see if you can all develop more stage presence.

> **Gaining and Maintaining Attention**

No communication occurs if a speaker doesn't engage and maintain attention. A great opening will immediately get the audience to pay attention. But, without additional stimuli, an audience's attention will quickly fade. This is why using active learning methods is so much more effective than teaching purely by lecture. (Five years ago, the National Science Foundation published the results of a comprehensive study that showed STEM undergraduates earned higher grades and failed less often when they were taught using active learning strategies instead of by traditional lectures). Of course, active learning methods aren't really appropriate for all formal presentations. But changing things up within a presentation can help maintain audience interest. Help your students experiment with the following:

> Use an unexpectedly powerful image.

> Make a humorous comment or tell an engaging personal story.

> Ask the audience to imagine something that relates to your presentation that will help connect them personally to the material.

> Move around the presentation space, gesture actively (but not wildly), and change up volume and pace.

> **Developing a Voice That Is Appropriate in Volume and Articulation**

Clear articulation of words at an appropriate volume that carries across the presentation space is an essential feature of a good presentation. Volume and articulation are skills that require practice; good muscles in the mouth, lungs, and diaphragm; and confidence. Especially good speakers can sound confident and authoritative even when they aren't actually sure of what they're saying. Of course, we should also teach students to be honest presenters.

> ▸ **Using a Microphone/Working with a Sign-Language Interpreter or Automatic Transcriber**

Many people do not like the sound of their own voice, particularly when it is amplified. How many large gatherings have you attended at which a speaker chooses not to use the microphone? This is almost never appropriate. Members of the audience who can't hear well aren't likely to tell you that, and it also makes the presenter seem unprofessional and even self-centered and insensitive. As a *Chronicle of Higher Education* writer recently put it in an article on using a microphone: "It's not about you" (Ramey). Add to this the fact that more public presentations are making use of sign-language interpreters and automatic transcribing programs that transform into print what a speaker says in real time. These are additionally complicating factors, and they will increase in the future. The Americans with Disabilities Act (ADA) already requires course materials to be accessible to students with disabilities. So anything oral should be available in a print transcript as well. As the technology becomes more affordable and easier to use, it will become more common. For practice, have students speak into a GoogleDoc or a Word file. This software is now common, and students can use it to become more used to speaking in a manner that can be easily captured in print. Gauging speed, learning how far away to hold the microphone (or how close to lean into it), and enunciating clearly are all important skills for good speakers to master.

> ▸ **Using Visual Aids, Especially Slides and Images, Effectively to Enhance a Presentation**

We've all experienced "death by PowerPoint," in which bullet after bullet of text is read at us in the audience, generating various levels of enthusiasm. There are many sources available for composing more interesting and effective slides, and most of them highly recommend bold images and minimal text. Help your students develop more fluidity in creating clean, compelling slides that use graphs, charts, photos, and other visuals to enhance their presentations. Infographics and data visualization are becoming more and more important features of compelling in-person and recorded slide show presentations. Garr Reynolds's *Presentation Zen: Simple Ideas on Presentation Design and Delivery* is a great place to start to learn more about creating excellent slides. This book includes tips on

- finding and including powerful images,

- how much and how big to make text,

- how to use color effectively,

- how to make an emotional impact,

- how to make statistics pop,

- arranging slides to create balance and excitement,

and much more. Just flipping through the book and Reynolds's follow-up, *Presentation Zen Design: A Simple Visual Approach to Presenting in Today's World,* is inspiring.

- **Mastering Body Language and Gestures**

Low-tech approaches to public speaking are still relevant, especially for in-person presentations. Poise (bodily balance and control), gestures, movement, and expression are important skills for all students to master. Knowing what body language denotes and connotes is important not only to assist a speaker in communication to an audience; it's also essential for assessing one's audience.

- **Using Technology to Record and Distribute Presentations Electronically**

Many presentations in the workplace are now delivered via the internet, either through a live portal or in a recorded format. Software such as Screencast-O-Matic, Jing, and Zoom make it easy to record short slide presentations (with or without the speaker's face shown). Students can create presentations at home, taking as much time as they need, and then share them with peers in class or via social media. This can be a real time-saver too, as students can simply watch three to five of their peers' video presentations outside class as opposed to sitting through an entire class set of in-person presentations. Delivery and viewing of these presentations can be done in small groups or as a whole class. As a bonus, they can also be easily shared with parents and school administrators to show others how advanced your students are getting.

▸ **Being Memorable**

To have any real impact at all, a presentation must be memorable. As Aristotle might ask, "What are the available means of being memorable?" Discuss with students why some presentations really stand out—and others don't. If your students can learn to make presentations that will stick in the memories of their audiences, their influence will grow far and wide in whatever field they choose to enter as adults.

Martha Sandven, a National Board Certified Teacher in Arkansas, has composed a speaking assignment for her students that they really enjoy because they are speaking publicly on a topic they truly love. Ms. Sandven has stopped into our Teachers' Lounge to tell us about it.

─── **FROM THE TEACHERS' LOUNGE** ───

TALK-TEXT-TALK: *Speaking in Seventh Grade*

Martha Sandven
Ramay Junior High School, Fayetteville, Arkansas

You know that you are doing something that works with seventh graders when kids ask, "When are we using THOSE notebooks again?" What is special about these notebooks? Students use them to talk their way into their writing and then write their way into talking, a practice that developed confident adolescent speakers in my seventh-grade classroom. I wanted to tap into the adolescent love of communication, so I tried strategies from the National Writing Project's College, Career, and Community Writers Program.

First, my department selected an issue with multiple points of view of high interest for students: video games. The text set includes academic articles on the benefits and drawbacks of gaming, informational videos, and infographics. This was one of many compiled on the National Writing Project's C3WP website.

To engage students in speaking activities, I wrote descriptions of twelve different characters, each with a unique perspective on video games. One character was an outcast at school who felt disenfranchised except when playing Minecraft, while another character's father was addicted to online gaming. Students would take on the roles and speak in character about texts they read and decoded.

On the first day, each student randomly selected a role and read about their character. In their notebooks, they wrote "Video Games" and created a T-chart with "my voice" on one side and "character's voice" on the other. Students named their characters and fleshed out their profiles (favorite music, foods, hobbies) in their notebooks. Students wrote about video games in their own voice for five minutes, then in their character's voice for five minutes. After writing, students discussed video games at their tables in character. I watched every student participate in discussion without further prompting. Students who sometimes dominate a conversation were better listeners as they concentrated on staying in role. When the timer buzzed, students cried, "One more minute!" After role-play, students updated their thoughts and claims about video games in their notebooks. We never spent an entire period engaged in role-play, so there was always more to talk about the next day.

After five days of students reading and writing from different perspectives, I assumed the role of a school administrator whose husband played games day and night. I presented a policy to ban video gaming on campus due to the harmful effects of gaming on gamers and their families. Students were to present their own claims about video gaming and banning in a town hall–style meeting. Using evidence and notes from their readings and role-play discussions, each stood and spoke for one to three minutes. They stated a claim, shared their evidence, and provided commentary to connect their evidence to the claim.

During the mock town hall, students successfully completed the speaking task. Typically, reluctant speakers will ask a teacher or peer to present for them; however, during this project, everyone participated. From then on, students were more relaxed about speaking and presenting. Through talk-text-talk, students engaged in respectful argumentative discourse, lifting their voices, expressing their ideas, and communicating with clarity.

A great resource for high-quality presentations that are also *about* public speaking is the TED playlist "Before Public Speaking," which includes brief videos with tips for composing an engaging presentation, using body language effectively, conquering stage fright, and more.

STRATEGIES OF TALKING

▶ **Starting/Accepting Conversation**

Many people have trouble beginning a casual conversation with a stranger, even if they'd like to. It's a skill to be able to be the first to speak in a manner that begins a new conversation. It's also important that people know how to make themselves appear open to conversation with body language and an appropriate look. Conversely, it's possible some may need to learn how to forestall casual conversation where and when it's not wanted. Conversation requires consent. Young people should learn how to indicate whether they are open to interaction. They should also learn to read these signals from others. Imagine students at a dance or a party. What body language indicates readiness for conversation? How can one tell if someone else doesn't want to talk? What are some appropriate topics for discussion with someone you're just meeting?

An especially skilled conversationalist is good at asking the kinds of questions that generate lively discussion appropriately. Ken remembers a conversation at a social gathering where a brand-new acquaintance began an incredibly funny conversation among strangers by asking, "What's the most disgusting thing you've ever eaten?" Not every question need be brilliant or lead to humorous anecdotes; a good conversationalist usually has the ability to spark conversation in others with an interesting question or a reaction that solicits engaged responses.

What do you think would be the most enjoyable job in the world? Are you more afraid of heights or snakes? Would you rather be able to breathe underwater or fly through the air? Here's a good source that offers sixty-eight questions that can help start a positive conversation (Frost).

▸ **Being Assertive**

Especially these days, it seems there's no shortage of people who use interruption to bully others in a conversation. In general, it's appropriate to wait one's turn to talk. However, the ability to make oneself heard is an important skill for professional success and for being taken seriously in any conversational context. In fact, staff at the Mayo Clinic even believe that assertive behavior can lead to reduced stress and better decision making. Asserting oneself firmly but politely is a challenging task for many people, and there are even occasions when it's wise for one to assert oneself even impolitely. It can be tricky to interject in a conversation among a group of people or with one person who monopolizes conversation.

Interrupting is sometimes necessary, and doing so effectively—waiting for a brief pause—is an art. In fact, in some contexts, interruption is expected. On the other hand, students also see widely publicized discourse events where interruption is used to great effect as a silencing and bullying tactic—something that we would want to identify but not emulate. Regardless, some people find it virtually impossible to insert themselves into conversation. This is a loss for all because quiet or shy people still have terrific ideas to contribute. A lack of assertiveness can even be dangerous, as there are times when an emergency dictates an interruption. It might be beneficial to help your students develop appropriate skills of assertiveness. Of course, you may also have students who already have this skill in abundance and may need to learn to remain silent and listen more often. (See pages 134–43 for more on developing better listening skills.)

IN THE BRONX, *interrupting in a conversation is not only permissible but expected. We say "Uh huh" and "Really?!" to show we are listening. And we ask questions along the way for clarity, and again as a form of welcome participation: "The guy who hangs out on the corner?" "Yeah, you mean on St. Patrick's Day?" We also participate by expressing appropriate emotional reactions or to add relevant detail as someone is speaking: "Oh, I hate that!" "I used to work there, too." We also tend to be an impatient people, so if we already know something we're being told, we may very well say something like "I know all about that. So what's the point?" Such interruptions are rarely taken as impolite—nor are they intended to be,—and in my experience it is equally welcome from women as from men. But not everyone is from the outer boroughs of New York City, and interruption, particularly from a man, is not always taken as a good-natured interjection. Nor, if I'm being honest, is that always what my interruptions are.*

Given my background, I find it a challenge not to interrupt, and I constantly work on suppressing the instinct. Often, I have to stop myself and say something like "I'm sorry I interrupted. Please go on." I also need to acknowledge that as a male who has been in a position of authority for three decades (as a teacher, professor, and administrator), I have probably gotten a little too fond of the sound of my own voice. So while interrupting is a native phenomenon for me, it can also be a habit born of other less innocent social circumstances.

I've tried to become more sensitive to this.

One strategy that works pretty well against my tendency toward over-interruption is when my conversation partner continues to speak over me as I attempt to interrupt. This helps me recognize that my inter-

ruption is not welcome, and it's not as overtly challenging as saying something like "Excuse me, but I'm not finished." Or, as my loving spouse puts it, "Let me finish, you [bleepidly] [bleeping] [bleep]!" I've noticed that some women have developed this ability to continue to speak despite interruption, and I think it's beneficial for everyone of every gender, including more reticent people, to build this habit so that they can ensure their contributions don't get dismissed—or remain unheard—even inadvertently.

According to a 2017 New York Times *article, "Researchers consistently find that women are interrupted more and that men dominate conversations and decision-making, in corporate offices, town meetings, school boards and the United States Senate" (Chira). Another source, from a post on the website* Bustle, *wittily calls this phenomenon "manterrupting," and offers ways women and people of color can "take [and keep] the floor" more often (Weiss). Acknowledging my own habits as a speaker in conversation is hopefully allowing me to improve my own skills and to learn more from those I communicate with.*

MOST OF US BRING *into our teaching the lessons and lore of our upbringing and family, and in many instances those lessons serve us well in the classroom. In my case, however, my family's horror of interrupting anyone's speech or comment became a real problem for me as I attempted to deal with large group conversations among my students.*

In my talkative family of teachers and lawyers, we were all mostly eager to prove our points and to make our argumentative cases. It was the family's best and favorite indoor sport. As a young girl, I was a terrible interrupter offender and would quickly blurt out my example, refutation,

71

or disagreement. The reaction was almost always negative—the interruption was greeted as rude and ill timed, and, if it was too egregious, I would be excluded from the subsequent discussion. This was harsh punishment indeed, but it was how my family conducted its frequent and contentious discussions.

Unsurprisingly, I learned how to rein in my eagerness and wait my turn (hard as it was!) to riposte. I carried this habit with me into later high school, college, and graduate school, and, naturally, into my teaching.

What I found, however, was that my students, often when they became truly engaged with whatever we were doing in class—which character was untrustworthy, whose poem was best, why I the teacher needed to change an assignment—talked loudly, talked over each other, and didn't necessarily listen to the opposing argument.

Actually, they reminded me a lot of me as a younger person.

At first I attempted to extinguish this behavior, linking such interruptions with rudeness, discourtesy, and general misbehavior, as I had been taught. Students listened, but it didn't have the effect I wanted, and at times my hectoring seemed to do the one thing I didn't want to do: stop the conversation entirely.

So I began to listen carefully to the pattern of these loud and apparently disruptive conversations. As I listened, it became apparent to me that what I had assumed was undifferentiated chaos was more a genuine and honest ebb and flow, give and take, where speakers jumped in to make a point not because of a lack of care for others but because they were engaged.

While I never stopped wishing that one speaker could finish before another started—old habits die hard—I absolutely stopped correcting, criticizing, and admonishing when every interruption happened. I think I

realized that my family rules, useful as they may have been for that little
community, could not work well in all circumstances, especially in a lively,
languaging classroom.

Interruptions? Go ahead, I say: within limits, they are the mark of
engaged speakers, not rude ones.

And now for a complication of the entire talking-interrupting scenario.

Ken points out in his story that the ways speakers and listeners act is often a product of a culture. The more teachers understand the cultures of their students—namely, how those students have learned to understand and value certain behaviors in oral communication—the better it is for teachers and students. First, teachers will be better at helping their students to value other oral communication spaces and practices if they can directly compare those spaces and practices to those students are already familiar with. Second—and at least as important—teachers and other students may learn new strategies from the students.

In her *Culturally Responsive Teaching: Theory, Research, and Practice*, Geneva Gay describes the "call-response" participatory discourse style common among African Americans:

It involves listeners giving encouragement, commentary, compliments, and even criticism to speakers *as they are talking*. The speaker's responsibility is to issue the "calls" (making statements), and the listeners' obligation is to respond in some expressive, and often auditory, way (e.g., smiling, vocalizing, looking about, moving around, "amening"). (119)

Gay also describes a "talk-story" or "co-narration" process prevalent among Native Hawaiian speakers that "involves several students working collaboratively, or talking together, to create an idea, tell a story, or complete a learning task" (120). This, Gay claims with support from several scholarly studies, comes from Native Hawaiians' preference for behaviors that better the well-being of a family over that of individuals. Similar to these discourse practices are behaviors called "cooperative overlapping" (Deborah Tannen's term) or "*rapport talk*" observed among European American women (Gay 120–21). In these cases, women talk along with a speaker to provide encouragement and demonstrate that they are engaged. Gay suggests that teachers pay attention to these methods of communication because they may differ from what some teachers consider polite classroom behavior. She also suggests that teachers might make use of these participatory discourse practices, provided they understand their "features, dynamics, and codes of delivery." Guy also makes clear that these practices are not like those that are proposed in some scripted curricula in which teachers are instructed to have students reply in memorized answer to canned questions (120–21).

And now we move back to our list of the strategies of talking.

▸ **Developing Comfort with Pauses**

Silence in conversation need not be awkward. Among intimates, silence can actually be a mutual act of love. (For a compelling literary representation of this, see the first pages of John Steinbeck's *The Pearl*, in which he demonstrates the loving relationship between Kino and Juana as they go through their daily chores while saying nothing to each other.) Conversants who feel the need to fill every space with talk appear nervous and can forestall more meaningful dialogue. Ask students about this issue; do they have friends with whom silence is frequent and comfortable?

▸ **Showing Interest**

All of us have experienced this: you're speaking with someone who checks their phone or looks over your shoulder while you're speaking with them. You wonder, are they looking for something better to do? An effective conversation partner knows how to look interested—even if they're not. Eye contact, phone in a pocket or purse, smiles and nods, uncrossed arms, and an occasional heartfelt "uh huh" or "really?!" can be effective in making the other person feel comfortable talking. Of course, focusing too much on another person can be just as off-putting as being ignored. Too much eye contact can even seem aggressive. Or downright creepy. Do your students have this experience with any of their friends? Do they have ways of dealing with this?

▸ **Avoiding TMI**

Giving other people too much information (TMI), or "oversharing," is a common workplace problem. As teachers we see this fairly often from students who contribute to class personal information that isn't really appropriate for public distribution. TMI often makes other people uncomfortable because they don't know how to respond and aren't interested in responding with a similarly personal detail about their own lives. Sending a private email to a special friend is one thing—even though the dangers of too-explicit an email are reported regularly in the news. But announcing private details about one's family issues, or discussing relationship problems, or being indiscreet about bodily functions, or sharing deeply held opinions about other people in a classroom context can be areas of concern. Avoiding oversharing or TMI is not necessarily something today's young people learn just by participating in daily life. It behooves us to discuss it directly, and our students can benefit from the exploration.

▸ **Creating Community and Intimacy as Appropriate**

On the other hand, the ability to create community or intimacy among a group engaged in conversation is a genuine skill. Sharing a good inside joke or a story can create immediate bonds in conversation. Salespeople and politicians are especially good at creating a relationship very quickly in even casual conversation. Some charismatic young people are also quite good at this, and their peers might be encouraged to see how they operate. Analyzing film clips of conversations among teens from famous films and shows could be useful too. Check out *Mean Girls*, *Legally Blonde*, *Stranger Things*, or *Love, Simon*, for just a few.

▸ **Attending to Pace, Volume, Pitch, and Personal Space**

Just as in a formal presentation, speed, sound, and position matter in conversation. There are some great *Seinfeld* clips available on YouTube that humorously illustrate the problems of "low talkers" and "close talkers." There's also a male character with an unusually pitched voice called the "high talker," but those segments are pretty mean, and some people can't help the pitch of their voices. There's also a funny "loud talker," Carl the Park Ranger, played by Andy Samberg on *Parks and Recreation*; clips of him are available through the QR code on the previous page (LeslieKnopeRocks). These videos, when treated with lighthearted sensitivity, can be excellent teaching materials for how to engage in ordinary conversation effectively. They also make the point in a safe manner so that individual students and their oral skills are not criticized or dissected.

▸ **Having Empathy**

One of the most important qualities of a good conversationalist is empathy. Identifying with one's audience is important for learning how to open and continue conversation and to determine how to respond to another's replies or body language. We all know enough people who don't seem to take any notice at all of their conversation partners' feelings. Clearly, this is something that needs to be taught. In particular, it's a good idea for people to learn that some humorous comments do not come across as humorous to all. A joke that goes over well in one situation may be a significant problem in another. It's worth discussing with students what kinds of jokes are appropriate in some places and what kinds of jokes are never OK: those that demean vulnerable people, or "punch down," for example. We could spend a great deal of time here exploring humor and how it works, but that is a task for another day. Yes, some mean humor appeals to some people. Among equals, or aimed at the more powerful, mean humor can be fun—it can even create positive community. But humor that comes at the expense of others who are already suffering—humor that kicks someone who's already down—is just bullying with wits rather than fists.

▸ **Sharing the Floor**

In a good conversation, all participants engage perhaps not equally but in a balanced fashion. People must learn how to speak enough but not too much. This requires being aware of one's audience and effective self-regulation. It may require assertiveness or restraint. Those of us who are easily able to talk and talk—and talk—can be frustrated by those who aren't as quick to engage. And those who are reluctant to speak much may be too willing to let others carry the water. Conversely, those who can't get a word in edgewise no matter how much they try often become bored and look for a way out of a one-sided conversation. The ability to engage in a balanced conversation is a social skill that may not be natural for everyone. It's helpful if we deal with this directly in the classroom. In fact, some adults could also use a refresher. Right? For a good example, *Seinfeld* comes to the rescue again with "the long talker" (just Google it).

Given these details about talking strategies, we hope you agree that what may appear to be obvious foundational parts of communication—speaking and talking—are actually quite complex emotional and cognitive functions. We think oral communication deserves a significant place in ELA classes. Once examined closely, the skills needed are more elusive and advanced than one might think. For that very reason, we veteran teachers are uniquely equipped to lead this exploration and give our students guidance on speaking and talking.

SPEAKING OUT/SPEAKING UP AGAINST CASUAL DISCRIMINATION

We mentioned earlier that assertiveness is a necessity for good conversationalists. Sometimes the need to assert is especially important. There's a great deal of attention paid to the media sound-bites from prominent politicians and celebrities. And tweets from the famous are now as likely to be reported as are statements at press conferences. However, most of us still get lots of our information, worldviews, and values from the casual conversations we engage in with family and friends.

Most people probably think of family, friends, and community as places of warmth, love, and supportiveness. And while we hope this is true for you, we also know that in some cases communities (even otherwise loving families) can be ground zero for forms of intolerance or worse. What does one do in the face of the occasional ethnic joke, sexist jibe, or homophobic comment when it comes from people we like or even love?

We may also witness the kinds of verbal insults that have become known as *microaggressions*: "the everyday verbal, nonverbal, and environmental slights, snubs, or insults, whether intentional or unintentional, which communicate hostile, derogatory, or negative messages to target persons based solely upon their marginalized group membership" (Sue). For example, a White physics professor might express surprise that an African American student did well on a difficult exam, a mathematics teacher might express the same about a female student, or a young person might describe a movie they didn't like as "gay." Male

77

students might disbelieve the athletic prowess of their female peers; females might scoff at a male's interest in dance or art. Such offhand comments are a problem because they "reflect the active manifestation of oppressive worldviews that create, foster, and enforce marginalization" (Sue). In another way of putting it, they "punch down," demeaning those who are already on the lower end of a pecking order or who act differently from a predetermined stereotype (there is further discussion of microaggressions in Chapter 7).

We owe it to our students to help them learn how to confront discrimination, especially when it arises in the informal groups they inhabit. But how do we approach the casual discrimination that may surround us?

Ken has learned from some of his students that a simple way to respond to something objectionable is simply to say the word "Ouch" and then move on. It gently raises a brief objection, causing the speaker to think (one hopes), and at the very least signals to others within earshot that not everyone agrees with the statement of casual bigotry.

The Southern Poverty Law Center, a bastion of antiracist teaching materials, has published the online article "Speak Up: Responding to Everyday Bigotry" that offers excellent, practical advice to those who would prefer not to let bigoted statements stand. The site includes gentle but effective ways to confront microaggressions and other problematic statements from parents, siblings, friends, and even teachers, among others. Their advice includes drawing on positive family traditions, seeking support from a respected relative, reminding others of the strength of their relationships, setting limits, anticipating and rehearsing, and more.

NCTE has also published materials to support antiracist practices, including methods for increasing talk about racism, such as the *Statement on Anti-Racism to Support Teaching and Learning*. This statement recognizes explicitly the importance of speaking out: "[A]ll educational stakeholders—policymakers, parents, and the general public—understand that they can best support educators or teacher professionals and students by actively participating in public conversations about racism and bigotry."

Educator R. Joseph Rodríguez recently published a guest blog post that demonstrates how well-crafted questions can open productive discussion about race and power differences even using state-required materials that whitewash history.

Students can be guided by teachers and teacher educators who practice critical
and multimodal literacies. . . . [For example, Rodríguez's former teacher]
Mr. Pettaway said, ". . . [W]rite down in your notebook what you believe the
historians Mazour and Peoples want us to understand."

Asking students to question the perspective of their state-mandated textbook allowed them
to understand that the book's authors—

and even other professors, curriculum specialists, and field test teachers in com-
plicity as members of the Editorial Review Board—favored inaccurate portrayals
and intentional exclusion of civilizations that contributed then and now to the
humanities—all across the ages and globe.

We encourage veteran teachers to read Rodríguez's blog for more inspiration and
ideas for responding to ethnocentrism in education.

WHAT IS ORAL COMMUNICATION TODAY?

Web 2.0 technology, the kind of technology that allows people to communicate with one
another quickly over long distances, has greatly expanded the forms of talk people engage
in today. No longer is a telephone the only way to have a conversation with someone at a
distance. Today, speaking occurs via the internet in several different formats. Let's explore
them.

VIDEO CHATS

Increasingly available software, such as Zoom, Google Hangouts, FaceTime, Skype, and
others, has made video chats as easy as they were on *The Jetsons*, the early 1960s TV cartoon
sitcom about a family living in the future, a time of flying cars and robot housekeepers. As a
consequence, meeting via video is becoming much more common in many workplaces. It's a
good idea to help students get comfortable participating in such chats and learning to work
with the media to do a number of important adjustments, including:

- ▸ Fine-tuning volume and picture quality

- ▸ Muting the microphone when not speaking

- ▸ Ensuring the background/backdrop of the setting is nondistracting and professional (Ken is working on this, as his bookshelves have pretty much declared war on him.)

- ▸ Moving out of the frame to sneeze or cough and more

One especially interesting thing we have found when we meet with a group of students on video is that it's much easier to read the students' expressions than it is in a classroom. See Figure 4.1 for a sample video chat. The nature of the medium is such that all the participants are looking straight into the camera at once, and they don't turn away no matter who is speaking, making their faces always completely visible. It's also much easier to ensure that students are truly paying attention—and they can see if you are, too. It's a brave new world out there.

FIGURE 4.1. Photo of a video chat using Zoom. (Photo courtesy of Zoom Video Communications.)

RECORDED, ASYNCHRONOUS CONVERSATIONS, AS ON VOXER, VOICETHREAD, OR OTHER MEDIA

Voxer is almost like a walkie-talkie on your phone except that all the talk is automatically recorded, so you can listen to the voices when you have time (see Figure 4.2). Then you can respond, and your listeners can hear your responses at their leisure.

Miller Place High School English teacher Brian Sztabnik, who has used Voxer with his students many times, introduced it to Ken. Mr. Sztabnik has stopped using the app for a couple of minutes to speak with us in our Teachers' Lounge.

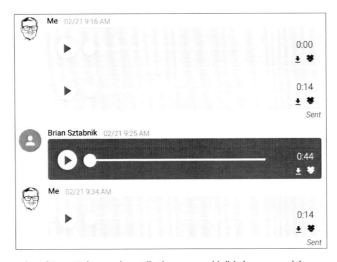

FIGURE 4.2. Screenshot of Voxer. To hear each contribution, you would click the arrow and the message would play.

―――――― FROM THE TEACHERS' LOUNGE ―――――

An App to Extend Class Discussion

Brian Sztabnik

Miller Place High School, Miller Place, New York

As educators, we know communication is at the heart of what we do. When we fail to communicate, isolation increases, understanding decreases, and confusion festers.

For years I have wondered how I could develop my students' communication skills while building their literacy levels at the same time. And then I realized the answer was in my own hand. I had been using Voxer, a walkie-talkie app, as a personal learning network (PLN) tool to connect with like-minded teachers. What I loved about it was that, unlike Facebook or Twitter, it was more intimate and personal. With Voxer, you hear the intonations, the pauses, and the bursts of excitement, all of which reveal authenticity, allowing more personal and genuine communication to occur. I was carrying around my dream team of colleagues right in my pocket, and I was communicating with them on a near-daily basis.

So why not try to create the same level of collaboration and personal development with my students?

I use Voxer with my classes to keep the conversation going and to push the boundaries of critical thinking. Voxer is a uniting tool as it turns my three AP literature sections into one group. Often, at the end of a school day, I take a question or an insight that arose in one class and pose it to the entire group. From the afternoon well into the evening, my students have rich conversations about the literature we are reading, taking the question or insight I posed and creating a rich and deep conversation, often in directions well beyond anything I have anticipated.

As my students are having these conversations about Frankenstein's character development, Elizabeth Bennet's conflict, or Langston Hughes's poetic perspective, their literacy develops beyond the four walls of the classroom. They are asking questions of one another for greater clarity and deeper understanding. They try to understand another's perspective. And when they present their own arguments, they validate their ideas with evidence from the text. It is what a rich, intellectual conversation

should be—full of challenges and assertions, claims and evidence. What
I love best is that three classes of sixty students unite into one cohesive
group where literacy and communication skills bloom in an organic way.

A different program, VoiceThread, allows a teacher to post a document on a website, and students can add oral comments about the document in answer to the teacher's question. For example, a teacher might post a photo of a painting and ask the students to state how the painting relates to a work of literature they are reading together.

Both Voxer and VoiceThread have many more features than discussed here, and they are great methods for engaging students in new ways of speaking and listening that are sure to develop further in the future.

NARRATED SLIDE PRESENTATIONS (LIVE OR RECORDED)

Programs like Screencast-O-Matic and Jing allow you to record short videos that show your computer screen and, if desired, the face of the speaker. These forms of presentation have the advantage of allowing students to take their time and record as many times as they wish before sending the final product. They can also be a real time-saver, as the videos can be watched from any device at any time.

Although it's not a technology per se, PechaKucha is a form of presentation that students might also enjoy. A PechaKucha, from the Japanese term for "chitchat," requires the speaker to speak without notes as twenty slides are shown in the background for twenty seconds each (six minutes and forty seconds in total). The slides are timed, so the speaker has no choice but to follow the strict format. In addition, the slides are images only—no text allowed, except as visuals (so, for example, a stop sign would be OK). PechaKuchas demand practice and obligate speakers to select powerful images that will enhance their words. Ignite presentations, such as those hosted at the NCTE Annual Convention each year, are similar, except they are even faster, using twenty slides for fifteen seconds each (five minutes total).

PODCASTS

If you haven't looked at all the podcasts available, you really should. They can be lifesavers for anyone with a long commute, on a long plane or train ride, or who gets bored at the gym. But podcasts are no longer just for listening to. Anyone with a phone can create a fairly high-quality podcast. National Public Radio (NPR) has terrific step-by-step advice for creating podcasts on its site: "Starting Your Podcast: A Guide for Students" (NPR). In addition to using their own voices, students can learn about ambient sound and about other sound effects. They can engage in writing, directing, and performing. Plus, as a change for teachers, you get to listen to and evaluate something very different from written text!

SOCIAL MEDIA PLATFORMS, SUCH AS TWITTER, FACEBOOK, SNAPCHAT, AND MORE

Perhaps social media is technically writing, but in many ways its speed and personalization make it seem far closer to speaking. As such, we teachers should consider treating social media as an oral medium, and we should explore the special elements of social media conversation.

To help us get started, many articles and chapters have been written on the status of facts (or the lack thereof) on social media, including our own chapter on social media in *Continuing the Journey: Becoming a Better Teacher of Literature and Informational Texts* (Christenbury and Lindblom). In addition to consulting that source of information, it's important for users of social media to be mindful about what they post. Social media "rules" are still forming, and there's been no codification, so it's difficult to give specifics. But social media technology certainly affords interesting conversations, especially because social media so easily incorporates visual as well as textual features. Many interesting conversations are about race and representation.

For example, a conversation on Twitter, primarily between people of color, was started regarding the newly available variations of skin color in emojis (see Figure 4.3). Responses to Davis's tweet include people talking about how they choose their shade depending on their personal appearance, their political stance, or some other personal criterion.

FIGURE 4.3. Tweet from Charles H. F. Davis III.

There have also been discussions regarding White people's use of darker-shaded emojis, and how they may be high-tech versions of blackface. Similarly, some White Twitter users have come under fire for posting gifs of people of color (often an African American woman wearing an expression of frustration or sardonic contempt) to express their own feelings. In some ways, social media helps clarify why some forms of expression are overtly political or offensive and why what may seem to be an innocent appropriation of someone else's identity can be seen as aggressive or insensitive. It's complicated territory.

Finally, we should also ensure that students are aware of the tools at their disposal when they are conversing on social media. For example, Facebook allows hiding comments, muting comments, and unfriending—all as ways to cope with problematic interlocutors. Other platforms have similar tools. Young people could probably use help in determining which tool to use under which circumstances as they navigate the very real world of social media discourse.

SPEAKING IN THE ERA OF WEB 3.0 AND ARTIFICIAL INTELLIGENCE

As expansive as Web 2.0 technologies are and will continue to be in the future, Web 3.0 technologies will go even further, breaking into new paradigms in oral communication as people increasingly engage with more and more powerful artificial intelligences. The chilling movie *Her* shows a romance between a lonely man and his artificially intelligent "girlfriend" that may not be as far-fetched as it first seems. As scientists develop more empathetic, human-like entities in the real world, humans will likely interact more and more with artificial intelligences in ordinary conversation. Ethicists are already asking questions about robot rights, anticipating a future need to consider practical ramifications of coming advancements in science and technology.

In 2019 the *New York Times* published a story suggesting that direct human-to-human contact may already be becoming a luxury for the wealthy, as screen contact becomes less expensive than meeting in person (Bowles). As an example, Bowles discusses the real case of an elderly man whose health care and personal well-being are monitored and communicated by a cartoon cat that is actually operated by people around the world. The ramifications of a screen-based life for the ordinary and an in-person life for the wealthy can be even more deeply concerning: "[A]s wealthy kids are growing up with less screen time, poor kids are growing up with more. How comfortable someone is with human engagement could become a new class marker" (Bowles).

CONCLUSION

Will the ability to participate comfortably and effectively in in-person conversations really become a skill lost among all but the most well-off among us? It's something for us to think about as we consider how to incorporate speaking in our curricula. We know, however, and believe, that the act of speaking is both a social and an intellectual skill that cannot be ignored or minimized in the English language arts classroom, and the opportunities to speak—and be heard—must be afforded to all of our students. In the following chapter, we examine specific ways to bring speaking into the classroom and to help you, the savvy veteran teacher, create spaces for your students to speak. This is a life skill that will carry far-reaching benefits in our students' lives beyond us, and it is worth our time and care to make spaces in the classroom for our students to converse.

Speaking in the Classroom

In Chapter 4, we outlined some of the major aspects of speaking (and talking) and how contemporary technology and social mores are influencing them. In this chapter, we bring speaking closer to home for English teachers by looking at ways that we can address it in our classrooms.

In some ways, speaking is a bedrock of English classes. Where else do students spend more time listening and speaking to one another in a semiformal environment? But, at the same time, we should make speaking a central skill that we examine and develop in our classes. Like so many practices of literacy, *engaging* in speaking helps, but it's not enough on its own. We veteran teachers must be clear about our goals for our students as speakers and how we plan to help them reach them.

TALKING IN CLASS: ONE EXAMPLE

Ken recently set up a class session that consisted entirely of students speaking to each other. The students had brought to class blog posts they had composed in answer to a question. The class was on teaching literature, and the question asked how the student had been or was being taught literature and what they thought about those methods. The students' blog posts were the materials the entire class was based on.

Ken broke up the class into pairs, asking students to meet with someone they hadn't spoken to one on one before; Ken knew the class well enough to actually be able to assign the pairs, but he could have let students make their own pairs. Then he asked the students to take fifteen minutes to talk to each other about their blog posts. In this case, Ken invited the students to speak to each other outside the classroom (during class time); in training situations, adults are often given the opportunity to meet in small groups in other rooms, and when possible, Ken likes to give students this opportunity too, as it helps them develop a more independent attitude about classwork. When the time was up, the students returned, and Ken asked each student to describe something interesting they learned about literature instruction from their partner. After the speaker presented their "take," Ken gave the partner (whose work was discussed) a chance to fill in anything the presenter might have left out or misinterpreted about their blog post. After each presenter and partner spoke (just about the one blog), Ken opened the discussion to the entire class, asking them to talk about what had been presented, and he did his best not to intervene in the discussion. Then he turned to another pair and began again. The class went through one-half of all the pairs and then re-turned to the original pair, letting the other partner give their impression of the other's post.

In truth, Ken did intervene in the discussion. But it was to redirect the conversation when it strayed from the points made by the pair, or if it was important for the original pair to be able to clarify something. Otherwise, Ken worked hard to resist the urge to give his own opinion. In all honesty, he wasn't entirely successful.

At the end, Ken said something along the lines of "Wow. You all really had great things to say about how you've been taught literature. Thank you! This gives us very firm ground to build on as our class studies how experts across the country and across the past 100 years or so have also thought about these topics." He then gave the students a few minutes to jot down any new information they'd learned (allowing for reflection), and the class was over for that day.

WHAT HAPPENS WHEN WE LET STUDENTS "OFF-LEASH"?

Often in class discussion, we teachers participate heavily, repeating or reframing what students have said, giving additional background or support to a student's point, or positively reinforcing students with a "good point" or "nice job." In some ways, although the analogy isn't perfect—and some non-dog-lovers may even find it a little insulting—it's a bit like training a young dog.

When teaching a dog to go for walks, a good trainer will use a leash as a tool to "correct" the dog when it goes too fast or pulls the trainer. The dog learns to avoid the gentle snap of the leash (the correction) and to receive a reward ("good dog") by staying within the leash's reach as the trainer walks. If the dog responds well, the trainer may trust the dog enough to do some off-leash work, such as coming when called, staying, fetching, and more. Some dogs never get off-leash, except in a fenced-in yard. And that's completely appropriate—for dogs. But dogs aren't being trained to one day go off to live a productive life on their own without their person. Students are expected to leave their teachers.

Many teachers, us included, often keep too much control in class discussion. It takes willpower and practice to allow students to develop their own flow of conversation. We must resist speaking too often, and students must not depend on us to do all the work to keep the conversation moving. The consequences of too much teacher control can be unintentionally permanent; if space is not routinely provided for our students and their voices, they will not continue to fight us for air time. Before we realize it, we may have made the classroom one where *our* voices—not those of our students—dominate. Allowing students to have such discussions and to build critically thoughtful conversation skills is crucial for an effective ELA class. There's no question that students should spend lots of classroom time "off-leash."

RESISTING THE URGE TO INTERVENE

Ken remembers a teacher who playfully covered her mouth with duct tape to ensure that her students knew they couldn't count on her to save them from silences during class discussions. We don't necessarily recommend going that far. Leila taps her closed mouth, and Ken extends an open hand to indicate to students that they are to carry the conversation forward. There are other strategies that can help too.

Before doing anything, you might keep a "stroke record" (using hash marks or other marks to indicate frequency) of how many students speak before you do. If you're like most teachers, it's often just one: a student speaks, you respond, then you call on another student to speak. Try expanding that ratio, even if by just one more student. It's even worth telling the students that you are trying *not* to intervene as often because you want the students to carry the conversation themselves. In the class described at the beginning of this chapter, Ken explained, "I'm going to try not to talk much because I want you to control the flow of ideas." For Ken this is a constant struggle. For Leila it is the same. Both of us work to enlist students in the effort. Try explaining to students the skills they are developing in conversations so they can consciously work on them with you. After all, doesn't everyone know how important it is to be able to converse clearly, intelligently, respectfully, and assertively?

A teaching colleague from Alabama knows something about how much teachers enjoy talking. Sharonica Nelson, an English education professor, is in our Teachers' Lounge now, ready to give us some advice.

─── FROM THE TEACHERS' LOUNGE ────────

Let Them Talk!

Sharonica Nelson
University of Alabama at Birmingham

How many times have you gone into a classroom where the kids were quiet as mice while the teacher rambled on and on? Unfortunately, heavy teacher talk *is the norm in many classrooms regardless of the type of school, the teacher's level of education, or socioeconomic status of the district. This appears to be consistent across demographics. Simply put, we teachers love to talk! Nonetheless, we should instead ensure that we hear more* student talk—*so that students too can learn (go figure), because whoever is talking is actually learning. Speaking helps students discover and shape their ideas. Further, it allows students to discover gaps in their thinking, comprehension, and understanding. As teachers of English, we teach the broadest subject area, and the most fun (IMHO!). Our*

content lends itself to rich bouts of exciting verbal discourse, and we must take advantage of it daily.

As an English education professor, I find myself constantly encouraging teachers to refrain from being the teacher who stands and talks the entire class period. I also remind them of the importance of teaching speaking, allowing students to speak, and even limiting teacher-led conversation. Teachers should be mindful of the importance of allowing students to practice speaking and to create spaces where speaking is welcomed and encouraged. Teachers should also model speaking while allowing students to experience formal and informal speaking through group discussions, presentations, and daily class conversation.

While encouraging speaking, teachers must also be sensitive to the cultural and linguistic diversity within the classroom. They can show sensitivity by accepting different dialects, accents, colloquialisms, and African American English. It is equally vital to model and teach about code-switching, code-meshing, and grammar in the context of speaking formal English when necessary.

The most important aspect of the ELA classroom is that students' verbal discourse is welcomed and valued. If English teachers are to truly teach students literacy, we cannot separate speaking from reading and writing. Reading, writing, and speaking each has its own role as it pertains to literacy. The three are a triangle that must be honored at each point for balanced English teaching. Reading is for comprehension, writing is for interpretation, and speaking is for articulation of the first two. The classroom should be a place for students to find, explore, and utilize their voices. In fact, speaking should be a fundamental part of the classroom culture and bolstered as part of a balanced curriculum.

Classroom orality is of grave importance for today's students who are thoroughly engulfed in phones and tablets, which causes speaking to

be overshadowed by texting, emailing, tweeting, posting, and back-chan-
neling. However, the verbal articulation of thought will never go out of
style. It is a skill that transcends the bandwagon of social media messages,
the craze of texting, and the impersonal nature of email. To aid in good
teaching of speaking, teachers should use effective strategies, including
fishbowl discussions, think-pair-share, literature circles, book talks, oral
storytelling, teacher-student conferences, and general student-led discus-
sion. Ultimately, speaking is the foundation of literacy and a skill that
lasts a lifetime. As James Britton so eloquently wrote, "[R]eading and writ-
ing float on a sea of talk" (11). Therefore, we must allow our classrooms
to serve as places that honor and hone speaking skills for the long-term
success of our students. Whatever you do, let students talk!

DEVELOPING A COMFORT WITH SILENCE

Teachers also must become comfortable with silence. As a veteran teacher, you are probably no longer nervous when a class falls silent, but the gap between comments still may motivate you to speak. Try to break that habit—within reason, of course. (We know of a teacher who said nothing for so long it became a contest over who could remain silent the longest. Hint: students virtually always win this game.) Teacher "wait time" can be a challenge, even for veteran teachers. Allowing at least three to five seconds of silence is appropriate. And if it makes students a bit uncomfortable, that in itself may motivate them to speak—and it may also give reticent speakers a chance to gather their courage.

If the silence has gone on too long, try cold-calling students, in a friendly way. And how can we make this friendly? There are specific behaviors we can adopt.

First, look to students' facial expressions for clues and use them as an intro. We often find that saying, "Alethia, you look like you might have an opinion on this," or "Max, have you ever had an experience like this?" can be enough to prompt a student to contribute. (In fact, calling on students this way even when they *don't really* look like they have something to say often reveals that they do.)

Second, it's also important to let students know they can say *no,* or decline to participate in some other way, when they really aren't thinking about anything particular to contribute. The point is to help students take the opportunity to talk, not to force them into a position of having to say something when they truly have nothing to say. (What an amazing world this would be if everyone declined to speak when they had nothing to say.)

Finally, we truly advocate that you avoid using cold-calling to catch students who aren't paying attention. When Ken notices a student who is not engaged, sometimes he'll say, "James, you haven't said much, so I'm going to ask you to join in shortly." This gets James's attention without putting him on the spot, giving him a little time to catch up before being invited to say something valuable. It's a courtesy of sorts, and it reinforces the collegial—not punitive— characteristics of the class discussion.

WHEN CONVERSATIONS GET HEATED

There are times when class discussion is serious enough to spark passionate emotion, and young people are not hesitant to express when they are annoyed or angry. (In a lot of ways, students are just like people.) In fact, many works of literature are specifically written to evoke emotion, often painful and disturbing emotion, and so it makes perfect sense that our classes would raise heated conversations. Social media and political discourse in general certainly seem to be creating space for, if not actually fueling, angry conversations. Perhaps one of the most important qualities we can help students learn is to cope with their anger—be it justified or not—and learn to channel their anger to energize their efforts to effect change of whatever kind they seek.

We take up the topic of anger in conversation far more thoroughly in Chapter 6 on listening. Here, we make just a few suggestions for dealing with class discussions that turn heated:

> ▶ Is the level of heat manageable? If you believe the students can remain respectful and are able to allow one another to speak openly without interruption or

shouting each other down, consider letting the heated discussion proceed. If you can, try to avoid allowing the conversation to end suddenly at the sound of the bell. Instead, give a closing statement, such as "We've heard a lot of strong points of view today, all of which I respect and take seriously, as I hope you will. Let's reflect on what we've heard and come back fresh to the conversation tomorrow." Such a statement allows the students to leave the conversation in the classroom, knowing they will have future opportunities to voice concerns. And they will be better able to move on with the rest of their day without being distracted.

▶ If the level of heat is unmanageable, it's perfectly appropriate to take a pause (or "call an audible" in the parlance Ken occasionally hears sports fans use, while he's reaching for a chicken wing). How can this be achieved? Teachers can:

   ▶ Use the whiteboard, document camera, or butcher paper to record the major points. (Sometimes paraphrasing them in writing can defuse their toxicity.)

   ▶ Have students take a few minutes to write their thoughts, and then use that writing to generate a more controlled conversation in that class or the next day. (Taking a day to think about the topic also allows teachers to get advice from colleagues or do some research. Yes, even we veteran teachers sometimes need help—and the good ones know when we need it and where to get it.)

   ▶ Ask students to take a few minutes to write their thoughts on sticky notes or on index cards and then use the notes (pasted) or the cards (exchanged) as records of opinions. Then resume the conversation.

▶ It's not OK to allow students to speak to each other in rude or disrespectful ways. If it happens, we must put a stop to it, and if the students are too angry to be polite, we must delay or avoid the discussion. It's also appropriate to teach young people not to allow themselves to be spoken to rudely. Learning to walk away or to refuse to engage in such a conversation—"I know you're angry, but I can't speak with you about this until you can be calm about it"—is a skill that can help students develop confidence and to avoid abusive relationships at home and in the workplace. It can also help them learn to deal effectively with authority, even if they believe they are being treated unfairly.

▶ If students get really angry, it's appropriate to have a conversation with a school counselor or another teacher who may know the student or students better than you do. It's also OK to ask the student, in private after they have calmed down, if they need anything. Without prying, a teacher can ask, "I know you got really angry during that conversation. Is there anything you need or that you would like me to know?" The student may disclose something: abuse, knowledge of a friend's serious issue, or another concern. As always, listen carefully to the student, avoid dismissing their concern even if you don't think it's important, and either refer the student to the guidance office or make a trip there yourself. Many times when a student acts out, it's a sign of help wanted. And, if the student says sincerely, "No, I'm fine," then all you did was make sure a student knew you noticed that they were in distress. That's a good thing too.

SEATING AND MOTION

The setup of the classroom, including the teacher's position in the room, sends a subtle but powerful message to students about their place. Are students passive vessels waiting to be filled, or are they active knowledge-makers, positioned to contribute? Rows facing a teacher in the front of a room is a clear signal about whose voice matters. Moving desks into a circle or into shorter rows facing the middle of the room can send an important message, even if it's just a temporary move.

It's useful for a teacher to begin a class by standing in a prominent place and gradually moving to a seated (or standing) position in some less central location in the room. This provides a visual cue that the teacher is gradually releasing responsibility for class discussion. Students have spent so much of their lives watching teachers that they are truly expert at reading such visual cues.

It's also a potent experience for students to stand up or even move to the front of the room when they are delivering their own thoughts. Ken makes it a practice to ensure that every student speaks from the front of the room on the first day of class. Often they are simply introducing themselves, or—standing in a group—reporting out from a brief group activity. The point is not to expect eloquence, but rather simply to signal to students that we all deserve space at the front of the room. We are all learning and growing and will be expected to share our knowledge with one another. Many students, especially when they stand in the front of the room as a group, also find this really fun. It sets a tone for the class: that it isn't going to be a passive experience for them, and that, yes, they also *own* the class.

AS A CHILD, *an adult, a student, and a teacher, I have never had a problem speaking. I grew up in a vocal, voluble family where holding the floor, telling a funny story, recounting a joke, or making a point were all prized behaviors. I was a star in that realm, and when I was older it served me well in my classes. As a teacher, however, I had to make a quick and permanent shift: my own oral skills often did little but silence my students, and the results of my verbal brilliance were not always appropriate to the classroom atmosphere I hoped to create. It was, in some ways, a sacrifice, to refrain from the appropriate comeback, to decline having the last word, to talk at length about an issue that interested me. But I quickly realized that despite the palpable satisfaction of my verbal ease and sparring ability, I contributed to the unease of many of my students.*

That was not worth it.

So what did I learn to do and then refine and somewhat perfect as a veteran teacher? Although preparing students for a discussion is crucial, both in content (what to say) and behavior (how to say it), much of what

I did involved my own behavior. To get my students to speak more and to speak at length, I:

▸ *moved from the front of the classroom to stand in the back or at the side, even when I spoke;*

▸ *tapped my mouth to remind myself not to interject in the conversation;*

▸ *refrained from commenting on or assessing every student answer;*

▸ *refrained from praising student answers;*

▸ *looked above students' heads when asking a question and thus avoided singling out likely student responders;*

▸ *made sure I scanned both right and left (I am right-handed) when I changed modes and searched for those who might want to speak;*

▸ *used student answers to encourage continued conversation;*

▸ *acted as though I didn't know the answer or answers to the questions;*

▸ *used significant (three to five seconds) wait time;*

▸ *practiced and used facial expressions of encouragement; and*

▸ *used student answers, without comment or correction, and recorded them on the whiteboard or smartboard.*

A well-run discussion with students at the center is often hard for early career teachers to unpack and also to model. Many begin discussions with their students and end them quickly, not understanding that it is rarely the students' fault that the exchange withers and dies or that, conversely, it disintegrates into mild chaos. With preparation, and in particular with the kind of teacher behaviors outlined above, a large-group discussion has a better chance of becoming the kind of exchange that makes the talk in English class worth almost everything.

WHAT IS GOING ON DURING A CLASS DISCUSSION

When students are engaged in a discussion, they are using their prior knowledge and developing new, critical ideas. They are inquiring deeply and using their imaginations to compose new thoughts. Often in a good conversation, students are thinking out loud. Consider all the skills students are working on when they are fully engaged in a good, critical conversation. Here are some of them:

- **Listening** closely to others

- Critically **analyzing** the information they are getting from others

- **Applying** those ideas to their own thoughts

- **Identifying** an idea of their own that connects to what they have heard

- **Articulating** a response that communicates their own ideas in a way that makes sense to others

- **Influencing** the direction of a conversation

- **Enhancing**, **supporting**, or **confronting** an opinion they hear

- **Asserting** themselves in conversation, **interrupting** effectively if necessary

- **Keeping silent** to allow others the space to speak, ensuring the conversation is truly an exchange, not a monologue

These are important skills that are at once intellectual and social. And, frankly, these skills seem like lost arts in many spaces today. Especially regarding controversial topics, effective listening skills and respectful, critical responses are endangered species. Yes, we know that many of us have been raised not to discuss religion or politics; but, in a democracy, the ability and disposition to engage in critical discussion—especially about controversial subjects— is essential. This concern is echoed in many opinion pieces shared today in traditional print sources, social media, and other formats: our classrooms are the safe places where students need to have these conversations, not avoid them.

QUESTIONS TO CREATE GOOD CLASS DISCUSSION

In 2016, Leila and Ken published the fourth edition of *Making the Journey: Being and Becoming a Teacher of English Language Arts* (*MTJ4*). The collaboration that began then continues with this latest volume in NCTE's Continuing the Journey series. In *MTJ4*, a book intended primarily for early-career teachers, we offer a good list of reasons (complete with explanations) why teachers ask students questions (Christenbury and Lindblom 336–37). It makes sense in this book for veteran teachers that we list those reasons, just as reminders.

WHY DO TEACHERS ASK QUESTIONS?

Questions are useful for many reasons. They:

- Provide students with an opportunity to find out what they think by hearing what they say

- Allow students to explore topics and explore points of view

- Let students function as experts

- Present students with the opportunity to interact among themselves

- Give the teacher immediate information about student comprehension

- Enhance the close reading of texts

All of the above are worthy reasons for asking students questions. If we keep these goals in mind, we veteran teachers are likely to raise valuable conversation and to avoid the kinds of questions (yes/no, fill-in-the-blank, overly complex, and vague questions) that tend to stymie a good class discussion.

Some theorists' work is particularly useful when forming questions for class discussion. Benjamin Bloom's taxonomy (and the revised taxonomy) spring to mind. Karin K. Hess's "cognitive rigor matrix" is also useful. In a book on questions she co-wrote in 1983, Leila devised a "questioning circle" that many teachers find especially useful as they develop questions specifically about literary and nonfiction texts or more general topics (Christenbury and Kelly). The schema covers a trio of areas—the matter, personal reality,

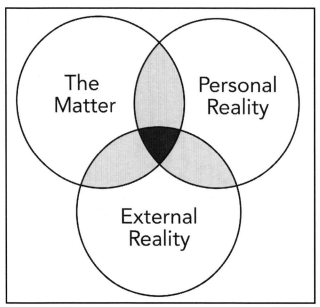

FIGURE 5.1. Leila's questioning circle.

and external reality. The matter is the subject of the discussion. Personal reality engages the experiences of the individuals involved in the discussion. And external reality is about other people, histories, and concepts in the world beyond the classroom. As the diagram in Figure 5.1 shows, the areas overlap in various ways, each of which can lead to different kinds of questions. For example, consider the following poem and the follow-up questions:

Cold Snap

The winter night in your face

darkened, and sparkling stars of frost

enameled your eyes. My words

caught on a splinter of ice

and bled to death. As their last heartbeat

sang to the music of the band

my ears felt empty and now

> I can't dance with anyone else
>
> with my blood frozen by your white hands.
>
> —James Hearst, *A Single Focus*

White Questions:

- ▶ Matter: What central image reveals how the speaker's words are received?

- ▶ Personal Reality: How would you define a difficult personal relationship?

- ▶ External Reality: What part does lack of communication play in relationships?

Shaded Questions:

- ▶ Matter and Personal Reality: In what ways are the poem's images appropriate for describing a broken relationship?

- ▶ Personal Reality and External Reality: Are your experiences with difficult personal relationships similar to or different from those of your friends? How?

- ▶ Matter and External Reality: How are the poem's images describing a specific incident applicable to a variety of personal relationships?

Dense Question:

- ▶ Matter, Personal Reality, External Reality: Which image in this poem do you think best expresses the complexity of difficult personal relationships?

Perhaps above all, it's important for veteran teachers to remember that the purpose of questions is to get students thinking. We know some colleagues who like to pepper their lectures with quick right/wrong questions, perhaps to ensure that students are paying attention or to allow students (or themselves) to display their knowledge. Questions such as "This play was written by Shakespeare, who was born in ____?" or "Toni Morrison's most famous novels, _____ and _____?" or "This poem is an example of haiku, right?" may keep students on their toes or shouting out one-word answers, but they also tend to distract students and focus them on factoids. It's far better to ask questions that generate complex, interesting class discussion in which students can use facts to stretch their own thinking.

THE VARIETIES OF STUDENT CONVERSATIONALISTS

As a veteran teacher, you surely know not all students react the same way to speaking in class. Some students are all too eager, while others might rather eat a bug (and not a delicious, chocolate-covered one) than say something in class. It's worth taking some time to delve into the different ways students respond to class discussion and how we can scaffold their efforts.

RELUCTANT SPEAKERS

Are all of your students participating in discussion, or are you really paying attention only to the few students who truly engage? In her popular blog, *Cult of Pedagogy*, Jennifer Gonzales refers to this as "fish-eye syndrome."

> It's a condition that impacts our perception, as if we're looking through a fisheye lens—the kind they use in peepholes. To those afflicted with fisheye, some students appear "larger" than others. They take up more energy and grab more of our attention, making the others fade into the periphery.

Most of us have to admit that, yeah, we've been there. We can do better at ensuring the other students are just as involved.

Many students are reluctant to speak much, if at all, in class. We are not writing here about students who haven't prepared for the class and so have nothing to say, but rather about the students who are prepared, do have something to say, but who, out of shyness, introversion, habit, or even phobia, do not contribute to oral discussion.

Would it be best for these students if we simply respected their personalities and allowed them to remain silent in class while more willing speakers carry discussions? We think *absolutely not*.

Unfortunately, we find too many teachers say *yes*, either deliberately or by omission, by not requiring all students to contribute to discussion. This is not a defensible instructional choice; in fact, we don't think it's at all appropriate to allow some students to opt out of discussion. If we allow them to do so, they are opting out of an intellectual community as well as out of building important ELA skills. And, yes, that said, some students require more scaffolding to develop speaking skills. We can't just *require* students into learning without providing supports.

But the good news is that there are strategies to use for reluctant speakers. These range from minor assistance to deep interventions, depending on the degree of the student's reluctance. Let's take a look at some of these.

Minor reluctance: Some students just prefer listening to speaking. This may be habit or lack of initiative. These students often just need a bit of prompting. Try asking, "Shana, do you have something you'd like to add?" "Joaquin, has something like this ever occurred to you?" If cold-calling a student is too jarring, try something more open: "How about we hear from someone who hasn't spoken yet today?" We often find that question remarkably successful, especially if we wait ten seconds or so and look around the room expectantly (yes, that seems long, but we need to offer space for students to think and respond). One caveat: Be sure not to focus on one particular student, as that can make that student even less comfortable about speaking. It can also help to ask other students to call on each other.

As another strategy, Ken often creates a rule during a conversation that a student who speaks must then call on the next student to speak. He encourages students to call on someone they wish to hear from, not just those who wish to speak. This can work well because reluctant students seem to feel less singled out when the invitation comes from a peer.

Strong reluctance: Certain students may find speaking a significant burden. This can come from poor experiences in the past, lack of self-confidence, extreme shyness, or self-consciousness about something (e.g., a perceived speech impediment, feeling flushed, having a "funny" voice). In these cases, it's often a matter of helping the student speak from a position of strength. There are a number of things we can do.

Try providing some time for students to write down answers to a question or some thoughts on a topic. Then ask students to share what they wrote either by talking about it or, if they must, reading their words aloud. Sometimes students feel more comfortable talking about other people's ideas. In this case, it can be helpful to have the students speak to each other and then have each student talk about what the other student thinks (as in the activity we began this chapter describing).

Another idea is to have students work in a team and then present as a group on an informal topic. For example, give the students ten minutes in groups of three to four to answer a meaty question about a text; then ask each group to present for two minutes at the front of the room. Tell them you'd like everyone in the group to say something. Even if you find your reluctant speakers don't speak at all, but just stand in front of the class, that alone can help the student slowly develop more comfort being the center of attention.

Extreme reluctance: Some students—and we have probably all taught some of them—are truly paralyzed as speakers in class. In these cases, it is appropriate to speak one on one with the student about why they are so reluctant to speak. Often these students know exactly why they don't want to talk, and they will express it to you privately. (For more information on this, including feedback directly from high school and middle school students, see Lorenz.) Regardless of the reason, you can offer private deals to the student as you try to mitigate whatever is causing their reluctance.

For example, you can ask them to speak once a week in class, and promise that you will call on them only when they approve. Suggest that the student use a signal by putting a book upright on their desk (or something else) when they are ready to be called on. Privately, you should positively reinforce their effort—a quick nod or thumbs-up after the student speaks, or a fist bump on the way out of class, for example. You and the student might even use a private chart to mark the success. Of course, you will want to raise the expectations as the days and weeks go by.

When dealing with extremely reluctant speakers, you may have no success or you may find there's a serious reason for the student's persistent silence. The student may be bullied and wants to remain invisible; the student may be a victim of assault and exhibiting related behaviors; or there may be some physiological condition that you can't influence. In these cases, of course, it's incumbent upon you to inform the school's guidance counselor, administration, or medical staff. These are situations out of our areas of expertise, so how you ask that student to participate will shift.

There is also the question of cultural background. In some cultures, some people are expected, at least in situations such as a classroom, to be more silent, less overtly expressive than others. We don't believe this should stop us from helping those students develop the ability to assert themselves, but understanding students' cultural expectations can help teachers determine the best way to encourage them.

Most of the situations we describe here are fairly common, but it's also true that many students become bored with class discussion if it's too predictable. Toward the end of this chapter, we suggest various forms of class discussion that can help energize you and your students.

Sydney G. Bryan, a teacher with experience in New York City and Long Island, has found several ways to encourage her students to become more proficient speakers, even if they are reluctant. She's made time to stop into our Teachers' Lounge to tell us about them.

───── FROM THE TEACHERS' LOUNGE ─────

Practice Makes Perfect

Sydney G. Bryan
Brentwood High School, Brentwood, New York

*There are two groups of issues that I en-
counter in my quest to improve students' speaking
skills: those rooted in self and those rooted in
skill. Issues rooted in self include embarrassment,
fear of failure, lack of confidence, and shyness.
Issues dealing with skill include fluency and lack
of content knowledge. Skills cannot be developed and improved until the
self allows it, but self often prevents students from willingly practicing
the skills. From simply raising a hand to answering a question all the way*

to presentations and public speaking, many students lack the confidence needed to take such risks. Speaking is not something that most consider a risk, but students who are aware of some of their own deficiencies in English often see speaking as a risk not worth taking.

How do we encourage students to take risks and invest in their speaking skills? Improving students' speaking skills relies heavily on practice, but what happens when students are reluctant to take even this basic step? Low-stakes tasks like raising a hand to indicate agreement with a statement or opinion expressed by another classmate help students build confidence on a basic level. Through such actions, students can see that there is some sort of consensus, and they are more willing to voice their opinions in greater detail. I frequently use "turn and talks" in the moments when no one is willing to volunteer an answer. As students discuss with their peers, I move around the room offering praise to those who effectively express their opinions and supporting those who seem confused or unsure. I might inform a more reserved student that I'll be calling on them to provide their answer to the whole class soon, thus allowing them time to prepare and also boosting their confidence for future speaking opportunities.

I also make public speaking a project requirement. When working on persuasive writing and argumentation, sometimes I assign the students to work in pairs to condemn or defend a specific character from our anchor text. The culminating presentations take the form of a modified mock trial in which students must present their arguments, acknowledge possible counterarguments, and refute their opponents' claims. This activity allows me to teach students how to effectively defend their opinions and inferences in a civil, informed way. We take time to discuss the differences between an informal argument and a debate, and we talk about why debate is much more effective. When it comes time to present, students are excited and engaged because of the opportunity for competition.

I model what an effective presentation looks like by giving a presentation of my own, and I provide students with specific ways they can improve their skills. Students are far more confident in their abilities because their claims are supported with evidence, and I give them plenty of time to practice and refine their fluency, tone modulation, eye contact, and gestures—all things that make presentations effective.

SPEAKERS WHO ARE CONVERSATION DOMINATORS AND OVERSHARERS

We have all also had students who enjoy talking a lot. More than we wish they did. What can we do about them? Most situations with extreme talkers are best handled one on one rather than in front of the whole class. We can sometimes get away with a "How about we hear from someone we haven't heard from yet?" as a signal to a talker that it's time to share the floor, but that doesn't usually work. That student will often wait a few seconds, look around at all the other hands that don't go up, and then begin speaking again.

In private conversation with an overtalker, we find two strategies work.

If the student is mature enough and confident, you can level with them and simply ask them to speak less often to give other students more of a chance. If this isn't likely to work, try telling the student you are impressed with their knowledge and willingness to speak up, but that other students are relying on them to do all the work. You need to engage the student by asking them to "help you out" by remaining silent more often so the other students must speak. One student dominating a conversation is not a good instructional strategy. You can reinforce the student's behavior in the same ways we suggest reinforcing the positive behaviors of the extremely reluctant speakers.

Oversharing is different. It's when students say things that are too personal for a public space, even one as semipublic as a class. Sometimes students put themselves in bad situations or see the world (even your classroom) as a much safer place than it really is. In cases like this, it's important for the student to learn about privacy and that making other people uncomfortable with the level of personal detail can be a problem.

This is not a cut-and-dried situation. What is too personal really depends on the situation. As teachers we must be careful not to dissuade students from bringing up topics that we personally find uncomfortable or inappropriate if in fact the topics are relevant and generally reasonable. At relevant times, students may wish to come out as gay, or disclose an illness or disability, or announce something about themselves that allows them to speak from a position of greater authority. It's not our role to stop them. In other cases, a student may have a question about a controversial matter but not have the words to articulate it appropriately. A White student, for example, may not mean to say anything disrespectful but may well say something racist or insensitive because they don't realize they are implying or stating something offensive. We can help students learn to ask questions more appropriately and more sensitively, but we should not silence students for trying and failing to ask a legitimate question in a responsible manner.

What can we do when a student truly overshares? There's no way around the fact that it can be extremely awkward. It might be best to quickly intervene and change the subject: "Thank you, Gene. Getting back to the point . . ." Or it might be better to express concern: "I'm sorry to hear that, Shanda. Let's talk more about that when class ends." A conversation with the student after class might well be appropriate, as might a walk to the guidance office to speak with a counselor, if your school has one available. In some cases, it's appropriate to speak with a parent or guardian. However you address the situation, learning what is appropriate for public disclosure is important for all students, and that lesson increases in importance as students age.

We have both had reluctant speakers, discussion dominators, and oversharers in our high school teaching, in college, and even in graduate school courses. These issues can remain or evolve at just about any age. Each new scenario brings a new dynamic of people together, and behaviors can emerge in unexpected ways. As ELA teachers, it's important that we help all students develop the knowledge and skill to engage responsibly in critical conversation. And that means sharing, listening, and, at times, editing the degree of intimacy offered in speaking.

ASSESSING CLASS DISCUSSION

Many teachers count "participation" in their grades, but do most of us discuss in any detail what constitutes good participation? Making the skills and knowledge of participation explicit can help everyone better build them.

Ken uses a rubric for class discussion, and he discusses it with students on or close to the first day of class. Sometimes students suggest additions or revisions to the rubric, and Ken happily considers them. See the criteria he uses in Figure 5.2.

The student . . .

---

1. responds to the teacher's questions

2. responds to other students, using students' names

3. makes comments that are relevant and generate productive class discussion

4. makes comments that incorporate valuable information from course readings

5. asks thoughtful questions and gives meaningful feedback

6. shows respect to others in the class

7. makes comments that take thoughtful risks (student reveals confusion, attempts suggestions to difficult problems, etc.)

8. shows an openness to the input of others and encourages or gives other students a chance to speak (does not monopolize).

FIGURE 5.2. Ken's class discussion criteria.

It is also a good idea to use this criteria list to create a rubric, working with students to develop specific elements for designations of "Excellent," "Very Good," "Passing," and "Needs Improvement." When students contribute to a rubric, they tend to pay more attention to it, and they tend to create a rubric that is more meaningful to them. Especially when class discussion counts significantly in a final grade, it is well worth our time to be explicit about an assessment rubric.

FROM *ACCOUNTABLE* TALK TO *RESPECTFUL* TALK

The idea of accountable talk has become popular with teachers over the past decade, and while we appreciate the principles, we don't like the term *accountable*. To us it smacks too much of compliance and the notion that students must be held to account for anything they say. For students, this can be extraordinarily discouraging when we teachers are encouraging an environment that should promote risk taking and experimentation.

Accountable talk also might mistakenly imply that the teacher's primary goal is ensuring that students speak *correctly,* which as we explained earlier is fraught with problems. It is true that speakers in life are responsible to many expectations when they speak (logical reasoning, community values, register of discourse, tone of voice, and much more), but prioritizing those expectations is a daunting way to encourage students to speak up. Instead, we strongly prefer the concept of *respectful* talk. In respectful talk, a teacher helps students show respect for each other and for the clarity of their thinking, regardless of their purpose.

USING DISCUSSION STEMS IN RESPECTFUL TALK

In a brief but instructive video, a teacher in Memphis, Tennessee, describes how she teaches students to talk respectfully to each other, requiring them always to use one another's names and to call on each other. Sherwanda Chism's methods are designed to help "students cherish their voices," which is a far more motivating and supportive goal than *accountability*. And Ms. Chism wants students to express their own ideas. "Everybody has something to say. We can say it as long as we're not harming and as long as we're not hurting."

Ms. Chism also uses what she calls accountable talk stems so that her students are learning to debate respectfully. We also find what we prefer to call *discussion stems* very useful, because they help students think about and then develop their own discursive pathways for engaging in critical discussion.

Most discussion stems are fairly low level, but we offer here some higher-level stems:

- "I agree with _____ about _____, and I would add _____."

- "_____ says, '_____,' but I don't think that takes into account the author's point about _____ on page __."

- "I don't completely understand why _____ thinks _____. Would you please explain that a little more or give an example of what you mean?"

- "I agree somewhat with _____'s point, but I think it would make more sense if we also thought about _____."

We believe that respectful talk achieves the same ends as so-called accountable talk, but it does so by prioritizing respect for the others with whom you are talking. Being honest, reasoned, and politely assertive are all ways of showing genuine respect while maintaining rigor in critical discussion.

SPEAKING ABOUT SPEAKING

One of the best ways to raise awareness about speaking skills is to ask students about their experiences and what skills they would like to improve. In fact, get students to present on those skills and take questions from their peers. These metacognitive approaches constitute one of the most interesting ways to teach English. We can read about reading, write about writing, and speak about speaking. We are learning and experiencing simultaneously.

What are some questions we can pursue?

- Do your students want to learn how to present information better to real audiences? Have them do some research on that topic and share it.

- Do they want to know more about giving political speeches? Ask a local politician or two to visit your class to talk about that; if that's too controversial, ask a retired politician or two from opposing camps.

- Do your students want to learn about how talking matters in business or in certain professions? Ask some professionals to video in to your class for a discussion about it.

- Do students want to know more about motivational speaking? Watch a video together and talk about the strategies used.

- Do your students want to learn how complex topics can be shared with general audiences? Have them scour the universe of TED Talks and select some examples to analyze.

- Do students want to argue more effectively in informal conversations? Have them do some reading in rhetoric and then practice the strategies in role-plays.

WHEN IT COMES *to speaking and listening, the topic of accents often emerges. For many people, an accent often has a qualitative twist: I don't have an accent, they will proclaim. Yet, for many of these people, they hear—and assess—accents in others. It is a consistent oddity that many Americans associate a British accent with erudition and high intelligence. Conversely, many associate the less popular, even stigmatized accents—such as those of my native South—with lack of education and, for some, with dimwittedness. (When native Georgian and 1970s presidential candidate Jimmy Carter campaigned for office, numbers of people interviewed declared early on that they would vote for him because "he sounds like us." For many others, Carter's southern accent immediately disqualified him from their vote.) Regardless, everyone*

does indeed have an accent, and despite predictions that television's wide-spread broadcast of a "standard" accent (often associated with midwestern speakers) would obliterate regional accent variations, to date this has not happened.

In my life my accent has, depending on the context, been heard as decisively "southern" (my students in Iowa had to occasionally stifle their chuckles when I talked—yes, I noticed) and aggressively "northern" (in my first semester teaching at a high school in southwestern Virginia, my assistant principal was wholly alarmed by my speech and asked if I was from New York City; the query was not meant to be complimentary). [Ken gasps!]

So what to do about accent? The simple answer is: not much. We pick up our accents largely from our peer group, and once it is established in our youth, it can be difficult to wholesale change the way we say words, in particular how we approach our vowels and our ending consonants. (For a somewhat different view of the deliberate, intentional change in accent, see Ken's story in Chapter 7.)

For some time, I have been intrigued by how English speakers from regions in the United States and also from India, Australia, South Africa, and other countries sound (accent) and, in particular, how they articulate certain English words (pronunciation). The variety is fascinating to me, and I try to keep a list of different examples beyond the routine to-MA-to/ to-MAY-to (tomato), a-GEN/a-GAIN (again), click/kleek (clique). Recently heard: inforMAtive (I would say inFORMative); DEEcisively/deCISEively; ACKumen/aCUmen.

Being fascinated with different accents and especially pronuncia-tion has come with experience. In years past, I believed I was tolerant and open-minded about accents and open to different pronunciation of words, but it actually was not so. During a writing class I taught some time ago,

I found myself routinely correcting my young students' pronunciation. I know language, I am well read, and the correction was automatic and made with confidence as well as, at least I hoped at the time, kindness. I must have overdone it with one class, however, as my students began to push back, claiming that their pronunciation was acceptable and should not be corrected. This was hardly a revolutionary act, but it was challenging to me as a teacher, and it was not a comfortable confrontation for me—I was right, and I knew it.

But what the students in this one class did was use an authority—in this case, a number of dictionaries—and, for the offending word of the day, cite first, second, and occasionally even third pronunciations. I had seen these distinctions in dictionaries but had never really paid attention. However, when my students wanted to use these distinctions as their weapon of choice, I did some investigation and found, most intriguingly, the reasons for these first, second, and third rankings of pronunciation, how they changed, and how they should be interpreted.

This I then took into class as a lesson; the students and I looked at about half a dozen words and contemplated the regional and historical reasons for the variance in pronunciation. At the end, I stopped correcting my students, they stopped arguing with me, and we all learned about the variability of accent and why words are said the many ways they are.

METHODS FOR CLASS DISCUSSION

It's pretty easy to find new methods for class discussion. Using them is important because changes in format will keep things fresh, will engage different students in different ways, and they are fun. Several good discussion methods also ensure more student-centered discussion, putting more of the onus—and the learning—on the students.

I ENJOY PLANNING *lessons that combine a jigsaw with a gallery walk.*

First, I split the students into groups. Let's say this is a class of sixteen, just to make the math easy; that makes four groups of four students (represented in Figure 5.3 as circles, triangles, diamonds, and pentagons). Each of those groups is considered an expert group, and each group is assigned a specific article to read on a particular topic. All the articles are related to that topic, but each group has a different article. The students come to class ready to discuss in their expert groups what they think is most important about what they learned from that article. After the students have discussed the article for a while, I ask them to take five to six large sticky notes—as big as 8½" by 11", when I can find (and afford!) them—and put one key word or image that represents important points from the article on each note and stick the notes on the wall near where their group is sitting. We call that their exhibit.

Then comes the jigsaw. The students in the expert groups each go to a different presentation group (as the groups of combined shapes demonstrate in Figure 5.3). At this point, each group has one student of each shape in it. Thus, in each group is one person who is an expert on each article. And each of the articles has an exhibit (the Post-its) that goes along with it.

Then comes the gallery walk. The presentation groups walk from exhibit to exhibit (one group at each exhibit, as shown in Figure 5.4), and the expert in that exhibit explains the exhibit to the rest of the students in that group, who take notes. After a prearranged time has passed, the groups move to the next exhibit clockwise, and so on, until all four groups have covered each exhibit.

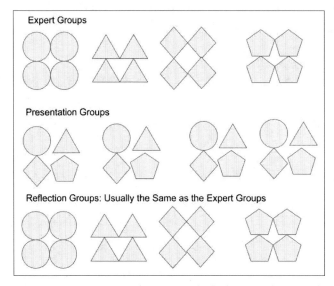

FIGURE 5.3. Expert groups, presentation groups, and reflection groups from Ken's class.

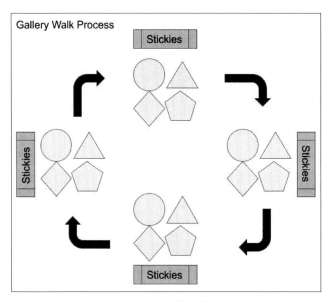

FIGURE 5.4. Ken's gallery walk process, which follows the steps in Figure 5.3.

Once all the exhibit presentations have been concluded, I usually have the students return to their expert group to reflect on either how their presentations went or what they learned from other groups (depending on my objectives for the lesson). This reflection portion is crucial, as it ensures that the students' learning stays with them. Sometimes I ask students to fill out questionnaires about the other students' presentations so that the presenters get specific feedback. I often then follow up with a new assignment that requires knowledge of all four articles. If all the students presented their exhibit well and took good notes on the others (with help from their peers in their expert groups), this can be an extremely effective method for helping students develop broad expertise in a topic.

Students mostly enjoy this assignment because it is engaging and social, and the students find the time goes by quickly. An additional benefit is that the key words and the key images use different skills. And it's also a relatively low-stakes presentation because it's done before a small group of peers, and I don't grade it (although I do assess students' knowledge of the articles later in a variety of ways).

Most classes don't have exactly sixteen students in them. Ken's activity also works with five groups of five or six groups of six. If the student count doesn't exactly fit, it's fine for one or two groups to have an extra member. In that case, the extra students share presenting duties with one of the others. The trick is always to make sure you have at least as many people in each group as there are groups. So if you have six groups, make sure you have at least six people in each group. If you have more than six, that's fine; just have the extras join any of the six groups. But if you have a group with only five or fewer members, when they give the presentations to one another, at least one group's presentation won't have a representative in the group.

So many other innovative ideas are out there for class discussion that it would be impractical to list them all here. Methods like fishbowls and think-pair-shares are ubiquitous. For some less common ideas, check out Jennifer Gonzales's "The Big List of Class Discussion Strategies" (which exists as both a blog post and a podcast). And see this list of Discussion Techniques for Active Learning compiled by Indiana University.

FORMAL PRESENTATIONS: TRADITIONAL AND TECH ENHANCED

Formal in-person presentations remain a staple in business, politics, nonprofit work, anything regarding education or training, and more. These skills, even older than the written word, continue to have influence and impact. What's new are the technologies for enhancing speaking skills: PowerPoint, Google Slides, Prezis, and more. Blending writing and speaking skills, oral presentations require disparate abilities, such as knowing how much text to put on a slide, what colors show up best, how images can impact (or even distract) an audience. Data visualization is an entire field devoted to making complex data visually simple and even beautiful.

Giving presentations will help students develop their voices (literally and figuratively) as they experience the power of emphasis, volume and projection, tone of voice (or register), well-placed humor, the use of pathos (emotion), and how to gesture and move to engage an audience.

Even newer to the scene are recorded formal presentations and informal video chats, both of which are increasing in popularity as the technology improves. We both regularly use video for formal presentations, for formal discussions (such as high-level meetings or interviews), and for informal chats with colleagues. Each of these situations requires nuanced skills that are not needed during in-person communication. For example, pausing is far more important in videos, as is knowing when the technology is failing and the communication is temporarily interrupted.

Programs such as Zoom and Screencast-O-Matic allow students and teachers to record presentations that include a shared computer screen and the face of the speaker. And there are many resources available for helping students compose and record their own podcasts. Two good resources include ReadWriteThink's "Podcasts: The Nuts and Bolts of Creating Podcasts" and Edublog's list of "50 Ideas for Student Created Podcasts."

As part of an education in public speaking, it's a great idea to have students deliver well-written historical speeches or even speeches from films and television. Such speeches are written to be delivered orally, and it can be a powerful experience to read—nay, to *deliver!*—a really effective speech. Students can experience how eloquence works by feeling the words in their mouths, can experience the power of alliteration and strategic repetition. They can feel how the sentences work with their breathing and their gestures. Even delivering just a few passages from a longer speech can help. And, since students can record themselves, they can deliver their speech in private and still give it in public, if for some reason that's their choice.

SPEAKING ON SOCIAL MEDIA

When email was a new phenomenon, it took people a while to get used to the genre. If you're older than forty, you may remember writing someone an email and then running to their office to see if they had received it. Yes, it's hard to believe we were once that excited to receive something that now, in the era of spam, is one of our great hindrances. At the time, the immediacy of email was new, described as something between a letter and a phone call. True to that description, email and then texts gave rise to less formal registers even in business communication, creative new abbreviations, and emoticons and emojis. Essentially, electronic discourse has ushered in a whole new age of written communication. Like it or not.

If email is like a phone call, then social media is like a gigantic megaphone. Facebook, Twitter, Instagram, Snapchat, and the many other platforms to come are so public, and information travels so quickly, that it may be more like speaking—shouting, even—than writing. Therefore, we believe that ELA classes should treat social media as a form of talk, and that students and teachers should engage in study of how those genres work and best practices for navigating them.

We know that many schools and even some state education departments block social media sites from classroom access. This, we believe, is a terrible injustice. Social media is a unique and extremely significant form of literacy. Neglecting to educate young people on its conventions, affordances, and consequences is nothing more than an abdication of our responsibilities as educators. If you, as a veteran teacher, face this issue, please connect with us and other teachers to help push back on misguided internet filtering. All English teachers need appropriate access to educate their students in social media literacy.

What are best practices for social media literacy? Unfortunately, we can't list them—because they haven't been codified yet. And with the rapid pace of technology, they may never be codified. So, rather than develop a set of rules for engagement in social media, we may be better off trying to develop dispositions, or attitudes, for social media talk that will endure as technologically enhanced conversation evolves.

Here are just some of the social media topics we think teachers should raise in ELA classes:

▸ What is at stake for me, for others, and for the institutions I'm a member of when I share different kinds of information on social media?

▸ How do I create a positive social media profile and presence?

▸ What do I do if I find out I have shared incorrect information?

▸ What constitutes cyberbullying? What should I do if I witness it or experience it myself?

▸ How do or should I respond to mean or insulting replies? What are the various options available on different social media platforms (e.g., unfriending, hiding, reporting)?

▸ Is public shaming a good thing? When, if ever, should I share posts that shame other people?

- What impact do images have?

- What are the rules for posting copyrighted information or images?

- When is it OK to post photos of people in public places?

- How are my statements on social media tracked and used by marketing companies and information research firms for various purposes? (There's a great deal of information available about Google Analytics, Twitter Analytics [see Christenbury and Lindblom 154–56], and other social media data-gathering programs.)

Please don't be too concerned if you don't have all the answers to these questions. Many of them are subjective, and much of the information changes rapidly. So becoming an expert in social media best practices may be a target that moves too quickly for any teacher to hit. Instead, we suggest taking an *inquiry approach* to these topics. Use them as topics for debate or research questions. Bring in social media experts with varying perspectives through their writing, videos, and even in person.

And don't forget to emphasize to your students that social media use does not mean you leave your manners and ethics at the door; the format may be different, but users also need to be responsible and civil. Even on social media, ethos still matters.

The purpose of raising topics related to speaking on social media is less to become an expert and more about developing appropriate social media dispositions. For example, we believe students should:

- Be very mindful about what they post on social media

- Be aware of the various ways in which their social media posts are shared with others; they should know about privacy settings and use them to control their media flow

- Care about the truthfulness of their posts and shares on social media

- Care about the feelings of others on social media and refuse to participate in bullying of any kind

- Be savvy enough to understand when they should report a problem on social media and assertive enough to do it

- Understand how to create a positive social media ethos that will follow them into adulthood

- Be prepared to address problems they have caused or false information they have shared

- Develop a thick skin and a tolerance for the flaws of others

- Be willing to engage in spirited, responsible discussion about important issues

- Make effective decisions about when to communicate via social media and when to explore other ways of communicating with one individual or many

- Refrain from using anonymity to engage in irresponsible social media discourse

Curse or blessing, social media is here, and it doesn't appear to be going anywhere soon. Our students must develop the intellectual and social skills necessary to speak effectively on social media. The ancient Roman teacher Quintilian is well known for his goal of creating students who are "good men speaking well." We may now wish to invoke him in our own classes as we prepare *good people tweeting well*.

CONCLUSION

Speaking up and speaking out are essential skills for our students, and as English teachers we must ensure that students develop the skills required to sustain themselves, their communities, and their world. An ancient art with astounding new technological media, speaking has not only remained a crucial skill but also grown in importance. Speaking to Uncle Alvin about politics, describing one's experiences to a potential employer, talking with peers to prevent a conflict or even a fight, reporting an injustice to someone in authority, wooing a partner, responding to a customer's needs, and sharing complex information in the workplace or school are all important scenarios for effective speaking. These are real-world situations—personal, philosophical, practical, and sometimes heated—that our students may need to negotiate.

Our students live in an increasingly technological world that gets bigger and smaller at the same time. We as teachers and they as students have the potential for far more extensive contact with a wide variety of people in the world, but most of us create and maintain very small communities with which we interact. And filter bubbles, social media algorithms, and engineered internet search engines encourage us to maintain our current relationships and resist making new ones outside our interest boundaries. Interacting responsibly with any outside communities can be a challenge with few established guidelines, boundaries, or recommended responses. And as veteran and accomplished teachers, we won't have all the answers for our students, but with our help, they can find the answers they need themselves to both communicate and to keep themselves and their privacy intact.

CHAPTER 6

Is Anyone Listening?

Listening is probably the most underrated skill in the entire English language arts curriculum. Often reduced to merely hearing meaning from voiced content, listening, we believe, is often treated superficially, if at all, even though it is one of the most important skills our students must develop. We further believe that many of the problems that plague us as individuals, as cultures, and as communities result from a lack of critical listening skills.

Despite its importance, listening is simply not as well resourced as the other strands in English language arts. For example, as of this writing, NCTE's ReadWriteThink site lists eighty-five grades 6–12 lesson plans and other resources for listening. This may sound impressive, but most of the eighty-five are either recorded interviews with authors or suggestions that students listen to a literary work via audio; there's not much on explicitly increasing students' critical listening skills. NCTE's well-regarded middle level journal, *Voices from the Middle,* published an issue devoted to speaking and listening in 2014. NCTE's secondary level *English Journal* hasn't had listening as part of an issue theme in at least the last twenty years, including—he admits—the five years when Ken was editor. To be sure, there have been articles on listening, and books that focus on class discussion also treat listening. But we contend that of all the subjects in the English curriculum, listening receives the least attention. Here we try to address some of that lack.

In this chapter, we conceive of critical listening skills in two ways.

First, listening is paying attention to sound, hearing voices, music, machinery, background and ambient sounds, nature, and more. Second, listening is working to understand, empathizing with what is heard. Thus, critical listening is deliberately setting aside one's own thoughts and ideas to learn more from and about others—and in the process learning more about ourselves. We take each of these important forms of listening in turn, defining and contextualizing them, and relating them to our work in English classrooms.

THE BASICS OF LISTENING

How do people hear and respond to sound? Like breathing or seeing, listening is an involuntary activity. Humans have mouths we can close and natural lids for our eyes, but our ears are always open; so unless we have a hearing impairment, we hear whether or not we wish to. Surely reading this, you can recall a time you wished you had earplugs: hearing a dripping faucet, a screeching child, a loud television, passing ambulances, frighteningly loud thunder. Yet we cannot always choose to tune out a sound even if we try because hearing is involuntary. This is certainly evolutionary, as the humans who could hear most perceptively were better able to avoid fatal dangers. But our inability to tune out certain sounds can be terribly distracting.

An ingenious app called Cafe Restaurant actually seems to work to block out the distraction of talk around us. In general, if we hear close conversations, our brains will work to understand them, even if we don't want to. You have undoubtedly experienced this when you've tried reading or grading papers in a busy space. Using background noise that sounds like human speech but that doesn't actually contain real words, this app sounds like a busy coffee shop but doesn't create distraction from overheard conversations. According to the app, "After a few minutes your brain will stop trying to decode the babble and the noise will recede into the background. If some real world sounds intrude, they will be heard as babble noise and will no longer pose any sort of distraction to your work" (Cafe). Ken often uses this app at school when he wants to keep his office door open for students who come by, but doesn't want general hallway chatter disturbing him. It seems to work. Why not offer this resource to students as a way to help them learn to tune out distracting ambient sound?

There are times, however, when we want to do the opposite of tuning out. In those moments, we can choose to listen *deliberately*: trying to make out what song is playing in the distance, listening to a radio specifically for a ball-game score, detecting whether a train we're waiting for is coming, trying to tell how much time we have before a storm reaches us. Choosing to listen closely, what some call "deep listening," is an important skill to develop and practice.

SOUND AND DEEP LISTENING

In an enlightening TEDx Talk entitled "The Difference between Hearing and Listening," Pauline Oliveros, late Distinguished Research Professor of Music and inspiration for the Center for Deep Listening at Rensselaer Polytechnic Institute, offers a compelling account of listening:

> The ear hears, the brain listens, the body senses vibrations. Listening is a lifetime practice that depends on accumulated experiences with sound. Listening can be focused to detail or open to the entire field of sound. Listening is a mysterious process that is not the same for everyone. Humans have developed consensual agreements on the interpretation of sound waves delivered to the brain by the ears. Languages are such agreements. To hear and to listen have a symbiotic relationship with a questionable common usage. We know more about hearing than about listening. Scientists can measure what happens in the ear. Measuring listening is another matter, as it involves subjectivity. We confuse hearing with listening. . . . To hear is the physical means that enables perception. To listen is 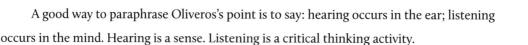 to give attention to what is perceived both acoustically and psychologically.

A good way to paraphrase Oliveros's point is to say: hearing occurs in the ear; listening occurs in the mind. Hearing is a sense. Listening is a critical thinking activity.

As English teachers, we might be expected to concentrate on listening to language, what Oliveros has called "agreements on the interpretation of sound waves." Before we make the turn to language, however, we wish to dwell on other forms of aural content. The sounds of nature. The sounds of the city. The sounds of a farm. The sounds of a suburb. The sounds of a school. All of these communities have unique soundscapes that are part of their character and ambiance. No matter how much we realize it (or don't), we constantly use sounds like these to orient ourselves and make meaning of our surroundings.

Jon Wargo, assistant professor at Boston College, has used sound innovatively as an element of multimodal composition to explore and empower students. In a coauthored piece, Wargo describes how he has taught sonic cartography (or sound mapping) to preservice teachers to help them better understand and engage with their new schools (Brownell and Wargo). Specifically, Wargo and his colleague used sound to help White student teachers better understand the diverse, urban schools to which they had been assigned.

For those unfamiliar with sonic cartography, it would be helpful to view an example; we found the Montréal Sound Map in Figure 6.1 that illustrates it. The site shows a literal map of the city of Montréal with green dots at various points on the map. Each dot links to a recorded sound from that space. Spaces include interiors of restaurants and theaters, outdoor spaces on city blocks and in city parks, and more.

FIGURE 6.1. The Montréal sound map. [Imagery ©2019 TerraMetrics. Reprinted under Creative Commons Share Alike Agreement and Google Maps/Google Earth terms of use.]

Brownell and Wargo asked six preservice teachers (PSTs) to create similar sound maps as part of their assignment to compose the community of their new schools. As the authors describe:

> It was the first opportunity for PSTs to intentionally immerse themselves in their new communities. PSTs were asked to use a variety of tools (e.g., StoryMapJS, screencasts, SoundCloud) to compose community using sonic cartography. PSTs did research online and interviewed their students, mentor teachers and other professionals in their schools. (4–5)

The students' projects included dialogue, ambient sounds, and more from sites within the school and in the surrounding communities, such as neighborhoods in which students in the district lived. By researching and composing these projects, the preservice teachers gained a richer understanding of the social and physical contexts of the multicultural schools. And they did so by listening and incorporating what they heard—literally—into their compositions. "PSTs were also asked to reflect [on] how hearing difference and listening to community through sonic cartography (re)educates the senses" (5). Brownell and Wargo finished their project optimistic "about the possibility sound and sonic composition have for listening to and for the stories that emerge and resonate in building community" (12).

A year later, Wargo published another piece in which he describes "how one youth, Andi, used mobile media and the affordances of sonic composition to sound out injustice" (14). Part of Andi's project mapped the sounds of hate she encountered in school and the places where she felt silenced as a self-described "queer Latina lesbian" (13). Using sound as a way to capture the experience of homophobia for readers of and listeners to her project, Andi was able to call out injustice and empower herself. According to Wargo,

> Sound is a palpable force in marking injustice. To witness educational inequity and personal injustice is, in large part, to hear it. To survive it is to have listened to it—and, as Andi highlighted, to have listened through it. (22)

Wargo's 2018 article is well worth reading, as he gives more rationale and advice to teachers for using soundscapes as a generative part of multimodal composition.

English teachers have used sound in their classes in many ways: songs that relate to literature, sound effects that work with literature, bird calls or musical instruments mentioned in literature. But as Wargo has shown, we can use sound in many more innovative ways to experience and understand atmospheres and cultures. This form of listening can broaden our horizons. Asking students to focus on these forms of deep listening may well help them better understand the value of close reading because they add great depth to what we take in on the surface through our senses.

I AM A GOOD SWIMMER. *Since I was a young child, I have swum comfortably in pools, lakes, the ocean, anywhere. I raced competitively in grammar school, and for one summer I was a lifeguard on a lake and even for a weekend on the Delaware River, where I pulled two boys out of the water after their canoe overturned and hit them both on their heads. These days, I still swim often, and the only courage it requires is when I remove my shirt in public. (I am really big and eye-piercingly white. If I ever meet someone named Ahab on a beach, I'm outta there.) Otherwise, swimming is simple and fun. But for the most part, I skim the surface, staying close to the air.*

My brother, Tim, on the other hand, is a scuba diver. He dons an air tank and swims down more than 160 feet in oceans and other bodies of water. He experiences the water in far greater depth than I can. He sees from fish-eye points of view, getting close to shipwrecks, petting friendly fish, or being surprised by nearby sharks (yes, it's happened), swimming through undersea plants, looking up from yards under water at the

*glimmering sun from above. I imagine it feels like flying. And while the
videos Tim takes are beautiful and fun, I can't imagine they're anything as
magical as the real thing.*

> *Listening can be like swimming. We can stay on the surface, hear-
ing what goes on around us. Or we can really listen by attuning ourselves
to the sounds around us, thunder in the distance and even the heartbeats
in our bodies. Like any critical skill, listening is something we can train
ourselves to do better, employing it to varying degrees when we wish to
for various purposes. As English teachers, it's important that we work on
listening with the same fervor with which we teach writing and reading.*

LISTENING TO UNDERSTAND

Of course, listening to understand—hearing words and responding appropriately to them—
is primary work in English classes, and rightly so. The ability to listen and understand language quickly and confidently in a variety of circumstances is a foundational skill. Listening
is also the primary means for understanding other people and empathizing with those who
have experiences we never will.

Veteran high school English teacher, department chair, and co-founder of the widely
influential #DisruptTexts website and Twitter chats, Tricia Ebarvia describes listening as a
form of social justice. We are fortunate that Ms. Ebarvia is in our Teachers' Lounge ready to
tell us more.

——— FROM THE TEACHERS' LOUNGE ———

Toward Justice: Listening as an Act of Resistance

Tricia Ebarvia
Pennsylvania

*Ask anyone what stands in the way of civil discourse, and you'll
likely hear that it's our inability to listen to one another. Now replace*

"civil discourse" with "equity and justice" and the statement still holds true: it is our inability to listen to one another that stands in the way of equity and justice.

While we teach reading, writing, and speaking, how often to do we teach listening? And I don't mean listening as it is usually applied in classrooms—as an act of compliance by students to the teacher—but the type of active, engaged listening that leads to deeper thinking and informed action. As with other skills, critical listening can be taught, and as teachers we can and must be intentional about making space in our classrooms for students to practice this skill, especially when it comes to discussions of racial justice. Too many of us in education—administration, teachers, and students—were socialized to not talk about race and to remain "color blind" to the real and lasting harm of racial injustice in our schools and society.

A necessary condition for building critical listening skills is a strong foundation in community. Providing students with consistent and varied ways to share their experiences early and throughout the year can help to nurture the sense of compassion needed to truly listen. This sense of community, however, should not be confused with comfort. *We cannot wait for all students—or ourselves—to be comfortable talking about racial injustice. We must recognize that sometimes discomfort (though never at the expense of any marginalized group) is necessary for growth.*

Before engaging directly in conversation about racism or other potentially difficult to discuss topics, teachers can provide students time to practice active listening through strategies such as a constructivist listening dyad or serial testimony, as practiced in many Quaker schools. In each of these protocols, students in the listening stance are not allowed to speak, interrupt, or ask any questions. In most class discussions, students listen not *to understand what others are saying but to interrupt with what they want to say. Consider how this applies to the common practice of raising hands. When students raise their hands, they stop listening; instead, they're waiting for* their *turn to speak. To interrupt this habit, teachers can do as educator Matt Kay does in his classroom and not allow students to have their hands raised while a peer is speaking. Students might also be asked to repeat back what they heard, without editorializing or offering commentary, in order to verify that they listened carefully and accurately. Teachers can also ask students to build on and connect to what their peers say; after all, you can't build on or connect to what someone said without actively listening.*

At the same time that we build students' listening skills and capacity, we must also teach students to consider to whom they are listening. Listening is an act of validation: by listening to what others have to say, we affirm that what they say has value. And so teaching students to listen critically also means teaching students to pay attention to whose voices are in the room and whose voices are not. Too often, students hear only the loudest voices in conversations: the pundits and politicians with the loudest megaphones and biggest pulpits. As activist and writer DeRay Mckesson has observed, people of color have never been voiceless; they have been unheard.

To resist the loudest voices, we can teach students to listen for others *and center* those voices instead. We can teach students to ask questions about who is heard and who is not heard: What is being said and not said? To whom have we* not *listened because their voice is missing? And how can we bring those voices into this conversation? Dominant narratives dominate because we don't listen to others. But by establishing protocols that ask them to listen critically, we help students develop the skills to question and resist these dominant narratives and to consider the* *perspectives needed in our conversations to build a more just, equitable society.*

WHAT IS LISTENING TODAY?

As we move closer to the mid-twenty-first century, the art of listening is, for a variety of reasons, a complicated affair. The development of cable television and the twenty-four-hour news cycle, begun in the late twentieth century, has resulted in media aimed specifically, curated almost, at those with particular political leanings. Internet blogs and videos have opened the world to any individual's pronouncements. Social media means that information—good or bad, true or false, politically interested or disinterested—spreads extraordinarily quickly across the globe. In short, there is so much information coming at us from so many sources that it can be genuinely difficult to hear much of it, never mind to listen to it closely for deep understanding. And making things more complicated still, it seems the most extreme views get the most attention. As one scholar cleverly puts it, those at the ideological extremes "are speaking in the town square with megaphones while the rest of us whisper among ourselves" (Mirra 2).

In addition, our social mores have become more complicated. Educators, scholars, social critics, politicians, legal analysts, and others have brought racial, gender, and class sensibilities to the fore. We are far more likely now to encounter discussions of White privilege, mass incarceration, wealth inequality, systemic racism, sexual abuse and exploitation, and the various forms of pushback against those concepts than we would have even just ten years ago. Basic questions about curricula—such as what authors should we teach—have become subjects of intense debate and critical thought. All of these debates and controversies stem from the fact that schools and educators are *listening* more closely to their communities and their colleagues.

Something else to keep in mind is where students do their conversing. According to an interesting PEW report from 2015, "79% of all teens instant message their friends; 27% do so daily[, and] 72% of all teens spend time with friends via social media; 23%

133

do so daily" (Lenhart et al. 3). Some good news is that 18 percent of teens say they "frequent-ly [experience p]eople supporting you through tough times/challenges" and 50 percent say they experience this occasionally (6). Additionally, the report points out that many teens—of all ages, income levels, and regions (rural, urban, suburban)—play online games that include voice connections. "These voice connections enable all types of communication through the game—conversations about mundane things, strategizing in-game play and trash talking" (45). Thus, even daily, friendly conversation among adolescents has gotten complicated by computer mediation and global reach.

With all this information and all this social change coming at us, when there is so much that we *hear,* it can be extremely difficult to choose what to *listen* to. In fact, we often tell ourselves we should "unplug" once in a while, go on a digital sabbatical, take the time to read a book or just talk with friends and family without checking our phones. With so much noise, is listening even possible anymore?

Such is the state of listening today.

TEACHING STUDENTS TO LISTEN

Given all the chaos, complication, and noise out there, perhaps it's not surprising that, as we have noted before, there aren't many good sources for teaching listening. Most that we have encountered skim the topic of listening and move quickly on to speaking. Even in this book, you will find more chapters on speaking than you will on listening. Ken recalls a time at a New York State Department of Education conference when a state representative explained that new, annual mandatory assessments were so important because "what you don't assess doesn't get taught." Moments later she explained that speaking and listening should, of course, still be taught, but they were not being included in those state assessments because they were too expensive to assess. And so it goes.

STRATEGIES FOR TEACHING LISTENING
LISTENING IN CLASS

In his humorous and helpful book *A Non-Freaked Out Guide to Teaching the Common Core,* Dave Stuart Jr. offers as a goal for students that they should be able to "[c]onverse effectively with anyone on the planet" (116). "At the most basic level," he says, "this means being socially intelligent enough to detect when you are bothering someone and to predict which kinds of comments or language choices may be offensive to a given audience" (116). Sometimes, listening means knowing when not to say something—or when not to say anything at all. Another strategy Stuart recommends is templates to aid students in speaking in ways that demonstrate they have listened. His example: "So and so, I hear you saying _____, to which I would add _____" (117). Focusing on listening in these ways has improved Stuart's students' "talking not just *to* but *with* each other" (117, author's emphasis).

In Chapter 5, Ken introduced his Class Discussion Criteria, a rubric that includes information about his students' grades. We repeat some of those criteria here because they are primarily about listening:

The student . . .	How Criterion Relates to Listening
1. responds to the teacher's questions	Students' responses reflect how closely they have listened to and understood the teacher's questions. How often does a student require a teacher to repeat? How often does a student give a response that does not directly relate to the question?
2. responds to other students, using students' names	Using other students' names is a way to show respect for others and to acknowledge that they have contributed something to the discussion. Asking students to call each other by name also encourages students to pay more careful attention to what they say. Students are less likely to make errors if they must attribute their claims to a specific peer.
3. makes comments that are relevant and generate productive class discussion	The degree of relevance of a comment demonstrates that a contributor understands the larger discussion. And generating additional conversation requires an attunement to the other people in the class.
6. shows respect to others in the class	Listening without interrupting inappropriately—cutting off another contributor—is part of showing respect, as is paying deliberate attention to the meaning of another's words.

8. shows an openness to the input of others and encourages or gives other students a chance to speak (does not monopolize).	Being open to the input of others requires careful listening, even suspension of one's own opinions, which is possibly the most difficult aspect of deep listening.

If you are looking for good suggestions for spicing up class discussion, Read-WriteThink.org is worth a look. For example, "Conducting Inner-Outer Circle Discussions" (Filkins) offers an interesting format for discussion and includes more good templates to scaffold students' listening skills. The Teaching Channel has some 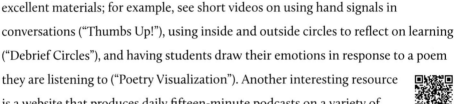 excellent materials; for example, see short videos on using hand signals in conversations ("Thumbs Up!"), using inside and outside circles to reflect on learning ("Debrief Circles"), and having students draw their emotions in response to a poem they are listening to ("Poetry Visualization"). Another interesting resource is a website that produces daily fifteen-minute podcasts on a variety of topics in science, art, entertainment, psychology, and much more (all archived and available). These podcasts are produced specifically for English language learners, so they are composed with simple sentences and are spoken quite slowly. Accompanying video slides include the text as the words are stated. For native speakers, it's a good idea to play these podcasts at a faster speed (just click the settings icon to increase playback speed).

Asking students questions—both about texts and about themselves—is also an effective way to build students' listening skills and to build important relationships with students at the same time, as Minnesota English teacher Jana L. Rieck has experienced. Stopping into the Teachers' Lounge, we catch a glimpse of Ms. Rieck as she makes herself a quick cup of coffee before her next class starts.

FROM THE TEACHERS' LOUNGE

What Questions Do You Have?

Jana L. Rieck
Champlin Park High School, Minneapolis, Minnesota

By the time you read this, I will have com-
pleted my thirtieth year of teaching and experi-
enced lots of movements and pedagogies—some
shocking, others annoying, most ineffective. I
have reinvented myself again and again. What
I finally learned is something that some of you
have known your whole career—it's not about the curriculum; it's about
the students. To truly be student-centered, to get students to listen, I ask
questions—all types of questions. I ask about their weekends, their post–
high school plans, the texts and topics they want to study, how they want
to determine whether a deadline works for them, and I ask many, many
other questions. Asking questions shows them that I care about them, the
barriers they face, and the struggles they may have with English. It teaches
them that they have a voice in all aspects of the class. Most important, it
allows them to take responsibility for their choices, to operate in the class-
room as they will be required to conduct themselves in the real world—on
the job or in a postsecondary program. The relationships I've built on
giving choices and asking questions provides me a doorway into the rest
of their lives.

One of the first ways I use questions is by discussing learning tar-
gets. Because of these learning targets, I am teaching students the skills to
enact choice in the texts we study. To further encourage students to listen,
I use daily agendas that show students there are spaces for questions. I
use technology such as Google Classroom, Remind, and email to com-
municate with them—providing them with information and asking for
feedback.

Since students make most of the textual decisions, their level of en-
gagement is usually pretty high. Sometimes their decisions result in bore-
dom, unhappiness, or struggle, particularly if they haven't made informed

decisions. They are willing to share because they know they matter. And
asking all of these questions gives me permission to ask them questions
about each text we study. For instance:

- ▸ *How would you describe Marjane Satrapi in the opening stories of* Persepolis?

- ▸ *What emotional burdens are soldiers experiencing in* The Things They Carried *(O'Brien)?*

- ▸ *Is it ethical to still study* The Absolutely True Diary of a Part-Time Indian, *given sexual assault allegations made against Sherman Alexie?*

- ▸ *Why does Rankine use a variety of modes in* Citizen: An American Lyric?

More important, my questions provide paths of inquiry for students.
They begin to ask questions of themselves, each other, and me.

In one specific case, all of these questions fostered a relationship
that allowed me to truly help a student. After having missed my class
for ten days, Don came to me before class started one morning, asking
if he could talk to me. I said, "Of course." What followed was a mono-
logue about how, once again, his family was homeless because of his
dad's mismanagement of money, how they'd moved three times over the
course of the last fifteen days, and that Don was feeling overwhelmed and
didn't have a clue where to start in completing his missing work. When
he finished his story, I said, "Don, nothing in this class is as important
as finding out how we can help you and your family." We immediately
went to see the school social worker and started the process of getting the
family help with food, housing, and transportation. Don came back into
my classroom and said, "Miss Rieck, can I give you a hug? I just want to
thank you for hearing me." I got the best hug ever and, while Don's family

has continued to struggle, I've been able to bring some stability to his life,

all because of asking questions and listening.

What questions do you have?

MORE STRATEGIES FOR TEACHING LISTENING

There are some other important moves teachers should make in order to ensure that their students are learning the importance of critical listening and are practicing and strengthening that skill. For example, when teachers are ready to speak to the whole class, they should make sure that all students are listening before they speak. Newer teachers can have real difficulty getting the attention of a class, and sometimes they just begin speaking, hoping the buzz from the class dies down. But if some students don't listen, the teacher will inevitably repeat their words, which excuses students from the obligation to listen the first time. Teachers should repeat as infrequently as possible. This doesn't mean refusing to tell students what they need to know; it does mean not encouraging students to ignore the teacher until the teacher gives explicitly needed information.

Also, teachers should encourage students to ask each other to speak more loudly if they can't hear one another. Sometimes students don't hear other students and they simply accept that. Establishing a community in which all participants want to or *need* to hear one another is critical. If you have students who are unwilling (as opposed to truly unable) to project their voices loudly enough to be heard in an otherwise quiet classroom, work with them. Help them learn breathing exercises so they can belt out words with the best of them when they want to—or need to. As we point out in the chapters on speaking, the ability to assert oneself is essential.

LISTENING AS BELIEVING

Highly respected composition teacher and theorist Peter Elbow has for decades been developing his ideas around what he calls the "doubting game" and the "believing game." Many of you may remember Elbow's doubting and believing games. To refresh your memory, these are methodological moves that thinkers can make to enhance their ideas and their writing. The doubting game is what we do ordinarily: we listen for flaws that undercut an argument or that open that argument to significant critique. The believing game is less common and harder for many of us to employ:

> [T]he believing game is the disciplined practice of trying to be as welcoming or accepting as possible to every idea we encounter: not just listening to views different from our own and holding back from arguing with them; not just trying to restate them without bias; but actually trying to believe them. We are using believing as a tool to scrutinize and test. But instead of scrutinizing fashionable or widely accepted ideas for hidden flaws, the believing game asks us to scrutinize unfashionable or even repellent ideas for hidden virtues. Often we cannot see what's good in someone else's idea (or in our own!) till we work at believing it. (Elbow 1–2)

We can think of Elbow's believing game as a form of deeply empathetic listening—listening with our whole consciousness, temporarily setting aside any doubt for the purpose of more fully understanding the perspective, ideas, and words of another. Elbow's work has been enormously influential in writing instruction, and we encourage you to revisit it or explore it further on your own.

Ken recently created a version of the believing and doubting games in his class. He calls it "Evangelists vs. Curmudgeons." For this particular class, Ken had assigned the students a selection of articles on using active learning strategies for teaching literature. When the students came to class, each of them picked an index card that had either "Evangelist" or "Curmudgeon" written on it. The Evangelists sat on the left side of the room and the Curmudgeons sat on the right. The idea was to have a long discussion (these were graduate students) about the pros and cons of the active learning strategies we had read about. Each side was given about fifteen minutes to prepare, and then we held the discussion.

Before the students went off to prepare for the discussion, however, we went over the rules for this game. First we discussed as a class what an Evangelist of active learning would do versus what a Curmudgeon would do (see Figure 6.2). Ken's class's sense of humor suited the idea of evangelists versus curmudgeons, but the game could just as easily be called "Advocates vs. Skeptics" or even "Believers vs. Doubters." During the game, students had to stay in their role, unless they wanted to—very occasionally—break their role to add something from the other perspective. To do so, the student had to raise a hand and say out loud, "I'm breaking role" before making their contribution. And the hand had to stay up until they were back in role.

The game ended up being fun, and Ken and the students had a long, involved discussion that was far more student-centered than a traditional, teacher-facilitated talk. There is no losing side in Evangelists vs. Curmudgeons; no points are earned and no score is kept. Everyone wins because all the ideas from the articles get a fair hearing, and all of the students and the teacher leave smarter than when they entered the classroom.

Evangelists	Curmudgeons
▸ Show enthusiasm	▸ Show skepticism
▸ Discuss specifics about what they value	▸ Give reasons why something won't work
▸ Give rich examples of what they believe	▸ Question the real value/impact of something
▸ Show their understanding of limits and explain why they are still advocates	▸ Use evidence to pose problems
▸ Are resilient in the face of even well-founded, challenging criticism	▸ Describe the limits of the effect of something, or show why it won't work for all
▸ Are not defensive	▸ Talk about times they've experienced the action and it didn't have the intended effect (didn't work)
▸ Listen carefully to skeptics	▸ Point out contradictions in reasoning

FIGURE 6.2. Advice for players of Evangelists vs. Curmudgeons.

DIRECTED LISTENING ACTIVITIES

Should listening activities be assigned as often as reading activities? The availability of podcasts, audiobooks, and other oral texts makes it easy to find materials. What can teachers do?

- Ask students to listen to texts of increasing complexity and length and ask them to talk or write in response to specific questions.

- Ask some direct, fact-based questions.

- Ask questions that require higher levels of critical thinking.

- And just as often as you expect students to cite evidence from a written text, ask them to cite evidence from an oral text.

Practicing and developing these skills will assist students in building skills they will continue to need in the future. In fact, shifting technology and the increasing number of oral texts available may actually make listening an even more necessary skill than it has been in the past few decades.

Taking notes is an important critical listening area to focus on as well, and not just as an add-on. There are many methods for taking notes and it behooves students to learn to use them. Nicole Mirra points out that debate teams use a technique called *flowing*, which she says helps students well beyond their debate performances. She includes a helpful template for flowing in her *Educating for Empathy: Literacy Learning and Civic Engagement* (113). "Flowing is crucial when arguments are coming at a debater left and right because failing to respond to any claim during a debate (or 'dropping' it) is a sure way to lose a round" (50). Among other works on note taking, a particularly imaginative approach can be found in *Ink and Ideas: Sketchnotes for Engagement, Comprehension, and Thinking* by Tanny McGregor.

We both enjoy audiobooks, especially in our cars because we live in highly congested areas with lots of traffic. Most books are read aloud by talented authors or by actors who bring such life and energy to the reading that it can be a true pleasure to sink into a complex tale or learn something new from a nonfiction text. Introduce students to the joys of audiobooks. Find some shorter texts and allow them to choose one to "read." Ask the students to deliver book talks on them just as they would books they read traditionally. Beware, though.

Ken assigns students to listen to audiobooks, and the students often claim they have trouble listening without falling asleep. In his honest moments, Ken might admit the same thing—although, luckily, when he's driving for a long time, a good audiobook seems to have the opposite effect.

In the ancient world, people could listen to poets and speakers for hours at a time. Yes, there was much less competition for attention; their version of Twitter was the town square, and their Facebook required human messengers—memes had to be acted out! Still, their ability to listen, absorb, and retain far outstrips ours. At least to some degree, it may be time for us to turn that around.

RESEARCH AS A LISTENING ACTIVITY

If you think about it, listening is finding something worth hearing and then focusing on it to best absorb it. In effect, that is exactly what any form of research is. Thinking of research as a listening activity may be helpful, not because we suggest literally using oral sources (not that there's anything wrong with that), but because it makes sense and can help you and your students conceive of listening as a more complicated and important activity.

Throughout the Continuing the Journey series, we interject the idea of helping students develop appropriate attitudes or *dispositions* toward learning and knowledge. We think the world would be a better place if more people had a disposition that favors listening. Listening is a learning activity. Learning is how humans improve and grow. We learn more about the people and the world around us, and we make better decisions as a result, as we discuss in greater detail in the following sections on empathy. When we teach students the importance of researching answers to valuable questions, we should explicitly remind them that we are asking them to listen to the knowledge and experience of others. Research is listening.

"LISTENING" ONLINE

Regarding the topic of research, we also need to keep in mind the impact that online search engines have on our ability to learn from outside sources. Our internet browsers very helpfully steer us to sources that are most likely to be useful to us. The software uses "cookies" and algorithms to predict our desires, and they can be disturbingly accurate. But the flipside is that our browsers also encourage us to stay insulated in our thinking. When we do searches, the search engine will provide lists in order of what we're most likely to click (and what advertisers have paid for). Eli Pariser has called these "filter bubbles" and "echo chambers," as we discuss more fully in *Continuing the Journey: Becoming a Better Teacher of Literature and Informational Texts* (Christenbury and Lindblom).

To combat filter bubbles, we should teach students first to be aware of them, and second to use more than one search engine to look for information. Also, if you read Twitter or Instagram or other social media that encourages vast numbers of public followers (unlike Facebook, which is best used only among friends or colleagues with shared interests), try to follow some people with whom you have little in common. You'll see a wider range of views on your social media feeds.

WHEN CONVERSATIONS GET HEATED

We discuss heated conversations more fully in this book in the chapters on speaking; however, we want to reinforce the importance of *listening* in heated conversations as well. A critical skill all people should develop is the ability to listen carefully to words even while those words are making them uncomfortable or even angry. Of course, there are some words and people (at times) that students should not be encouraged to listen to—we talk more about that later—but in general, it's important to be able to bracket one's objection or anger enough to actually listen to what others are saying. This can be a practical response: Sometimes we're wrong about what we think we're hearing. Sometimes we get a better perspective on our views. Other times we may come to better understand the flaws in other people's thinking. But if we are unable to listen as a result of our own emotions, that's likely only to limit us.

It's also important to teach students to "listen" to their audiences. Are people tensing up as you speak to them? Are their mouths tightening, are they frowning, shaking their heads, looking away, shifting their position? Are they looking down, clenching their hands?

It's no fun making someone angry without intending to. Most teachers have experienced having students get unexpectedly angry or emotional during a conversation. It's also important that students be aware of these reactions. Recognizing this isn't just important in teaching scenarios. Listening while speaking is a complex and essential skill.

LISTENING AS EMPATHIZING

Most English teachers would agree that empathy, the ability to understand and share the feelings of others, is one of the most important attributes that students can develop from reading literature and listening to the voices and perspectives of others. What teacher's emotions haven't stirred reading Atticus Finch say in *To Kill a Mockingbird,* "You never really understand a person until you . . . climb into his skin and walk around in it"? We use empathy as a rationale for teaching books from many different cultures, and it is empathy we are invoking when we claim we use literature as a window. Empathy is a goal for listening as well. Conversations are more productive, presentations are more inspiring, social action is more effective; legislation and policy are more fair when we employ empathy widely.

In her recent Netflix comedy special, *Wanda Sykes: Not Normal*, the comedian invokes empathy when she suggests that all White people "need a Black friend." Though she inflects her points with humor, her advice is serious. Sykes's impetus for the statement is that the television show *Naked and Afraid* (a reality TV survival show) booked only one Black person in the entire season, and he was a homeless man. "That tells me," Sykes says, "that there was no Black people in the room. When they made that decision, a Black person was not present." Other recent corporate decisions have prompted people of color to suggest that there aren't diverse voices at the tables of power, which limits the possibility for empathy. Possibly the most infamous was when Gucci manufactured a sweater that resembles blackface (Holcombe). Memes of groups of male legislators go viral when they make decisions about women's reproductive health and there are no women at the table. To come even closer to home, teachers often feel that policy decisions about the specifics of classrooms and school decisions must include the input of teachers—and they often do not, as they can be made solely by legislators and business representatives.

And lest this discussion seems a bit out there, we think it is important to note that empathy is an essential part of a culture that seeks equity and fairness across all races, genders, religions, regions, orientations, abilities, and classes. Empathy is a foundational quality for democracy and the most basic of patriotic American values.

Despite the obvious importance of developing empathy as a part of listening and reading skills, the concept is rarely mentioned in curriculum standards. Neither the 20-page *New York State Next Generation Learning Standards for Literacy in History/Social Studies, Science and Technical Subjects Grades 6–12* (New York State Education Department) nor the 127-page *New York State Next Generation English Language Arts Learning Standards P–12* (New York State Education Department) mentions *empathy* even once. NCTE and International Reading Association's *Standards for the English Language Arts* does not mention empathy. Nor does the *Framework for Success in Postsecondary Writing* copublished by the Council of Writing Program Administrators, NCTE, and the National Writing Project. "NCTE/NCATE Standards for Initial Preparation of Teachers of Secondary English Language Arts, Grades 7–12" is also silent on the subject.

A heartening exception is the *English Language Arts Standards for Teachers of Students Ages 11–18+,* Third Edition, published by the National Board for Professional Teaching Standards, which mentions *empathy* four times in its 107 pages:

- "Through reading, people connect to eternity and to each other. Readers can transcend the limitations of the immediate; they can empathize with characters from remote time periods and distant countries." (12)

- "Accomplished English language arts teachers structure activities to encourage students to listen with appreciation, critical awareness, and empathy." (64)

- "Teachers also build community by sensitizing classmates to the challenges of their peers and suggesting ways to empathetically support their efforts." (66)

- "Accomplished English language arts teachers understand that inquiry builds the disposition to evaluate different viewpoints through critical eyes and ears and to see the big picture. Teachers help students use the results of their inquiry to empathize and to find value in what others might find odd, alien, or implausible." (79)

We use these standards to remind ourselves of the many ways we can build empathy into our classes and how important listening is as a skill of empathy. In fact, empathy can be deliberately employed to diffuse difficult situations. Kia Jane Richmond, a former high school English teacher and author of *Mental Illness in Young Adult Literature: Exploring Real Struggles through Fictional Characters*, has used "empathetic listening" with students over the years of her career as an English teacher educator. We find Dr. Richmond taking an extremely rare moment to sit still in our Teachers' Lounge.

— FROM THE TEACHERS' LOUNGE —

Empathetic Listening

Kia Jane Richmond
Northern Michigan University, Marquette, Michigan

Whether working with a student teacher who is transitioning from college student to English teacher or helping a veteran teacher, using Carl Rogers's principles of effective communication can improve conversations about teaching. In 1961, Rogers identified three necessary components for communicating in helping relationships: congruence (being authentic); unconditional positive regard (having an accepting attitude); and empathetic listening, "grasp[ing] the moment-to-moment experiencing which occurs in the inner world" of the speaker without focusing on our own experiences (On Becoming 62–63).

When a student or colleague comes to us with a problem or question, we can use empathetic listening to focus on the message without our own agenda taking up space in the conversation. Taking notes while the speaker shares can help us focus on what is being said rather than what we might say in response. Restating main points to the speaker to check for understanding before responding is key to empathetic listening.

I have used empathetic listening with success when helping student teachers and their cooperating teachers to collaborate more effectively. For example, cooperating teacher Elaine was concerned because her student teacher, Christie, was not preparing detailed lesson plans in advance as requested. When I conferenced with Christie, she took responsibility for not being prepared but also shared "not feeling trusted" by Elaine. Christie said Elaine was still "hovering in the back" and moving around helping students during Christie's instruction. Elaine's actions, I learned, made Christie feel like she wasn't a "real teacher."

After I summarized Christie's statements to her, I spoke with Elaine. In addition to having concerns that Christie wasn't taking planning seriously, Elaine also admitted having fears about leaving Christie alone with students because of forthcoming standardized tests, the scores from which would count toward Elaine's annual evaluation. I summarized Elaine's comments, checking for understanding, then offered to videotape Christie teaching without Elaine in the room. Watching the videos, Elaine discovered that Christie was quite competent in her teaching and management of the class, which somewhat eased her fears.

Last, I asked Elaine and Christie to speak authentically about their anxieties and encouraged them to use empathetic listening before developing potential solutions. When I visited their classroom a few weeks later, both noted that they were dialoguing more consistently and that their relationship had improved. Christie had really stepped up her lesson planning. Moreover, Elaine was giving her more freedom to teach without hovering or intervening.

Finding ways to use empathetic listening (along with congruence and unconditional positive regard) can bring teaching colleagues closer and help them feel heard. Carl Rogers reminds us that whether someone is "hurting, confused, troubled, anxious, alienated, terrified; or when he or she is doubtful of self-worth, uncertain to identity," using empathetic listening can generate insight and provide support within the relationship ("Empathetic" 8–9). I encourage fellow teachers to listen carefully, take notes, and check for understanding when speaking; building empathy helps us create positive relationships with one another. Furthermore, we can extend the use of empathetic listening to our classrooms, which can also help us understand our students more completely too.

In her groundbreaking and 2018 David H. Russell Award for Distinguished Research in the Teaching of English–winning book, *Educating for Empathy: Literacy Learning and Civic Engagement*, Nicole Mirra pushes us to strive for more impactful forms of empathy, moving from individual empathy to what she calls "critical civic empathy." Mirra presents a brilliantly simple Typology of Empathy that has two forces that undergird critical civic empathy: Motivated by Mutual Humanization and Oriented toward Social/Political Action. If one is motivated only by humanization but not oriented toward social/political action, then one is exhibiting only Individual Empathy. Mirra's highest form of empathy, Critical Civic Empathy, requires that we also work toward social justice (7–11). Many in the field of teacher education agree. The most recent version of "NCTE/NCATE Standards for Initial Preparation of Teachers of Secondary English Language Arts, Grades 7–12" includes a standard (one of seven) devoted entirely to knowledge of social justice, diversity, and equity. Bluntly put, when we teach critical listening, we should be aware that we are also teaching students to be sensitive to injustice, and we should encourage students to pursue these ideals in their communities.

WHEN NOT TO LISTEN AND THE LIMITS OF EMPATHY

Language can be extremely seductive. We spend our careers trying to show students how language can be used to persuade people to take action. We analyze speeches, television commercials, and pop-up ads to help students understand how rhetoric works on them. We read story after story about people who have been fooled into taking some action that will haunt them, or even kill them. Learning when NOT to listen and how not to listen can be as important as learning to listen.

For example, young people need to learn to ignore taunting and mild bullying. They need to be able to eschew bad advice and those who encourage greed, jealousy, or pessimism. And they need to be able to withstand the toxicity of negative peer pressure. Role-plays and fictional scenarios can assist students in developing these skills. Older adolescents and adults need to ensure they can resist destructive persuasion, such as pressure to join in bullying someone, have sex without a condom, engage in petty theft, drive while impaired, experiment with drugs, destroy property, participate in malicious gossip, etc. These may not be situations you take up directly with your students, but certainly many of your students will experience them and will need critical listening skills to know a bad idea when they hear it.

Regarding more public discourse, some information out there is just patently false, and we need to be critical as we encounter it so that we can be prepared to disassemble it or dismiss it, as necessary. It is no revelation to you, savvy veteran teacher and reader, that an entire industry has grown up around the idea of producing "fake news" or "disinformation" deliberately intended to sow discord, much of it composed by so-called "click farms" and spread by "bots" on social media. With each *like* or *share*, we help spread misinformation like an epidemic to millions of other users. Platforms such as Facebook and Twitter are working to reduce the numbers of fake accounts, but there will probably never be a time when a platform is ahead of those seeking to deliver false information. We all need to be made aware of this situation and be ready to combat it. As teachers we need to bring this understanding into our classrooms.

In their book *Like War: The Weaponization of Social Media*, P. W. Singer and Emerson Brooking briefly survey the history of disinformation in wartime, and they reveal, frankly, shocking information about how false information is currently making its way to the American consciousness through social media. There's a fascinating oral interview and accom-

panying written transcript with the authors available at the National Public Radio website (Davies). According to Singer and Brooking, "sock puppets" are people paid to send out false information and interact with anyone who engages with it. And bots are algorithmically programmed accounts that can compose and share information, as well as use artificial intelligence to engage in discussion (although not well). There are also bots that create more bots.

> The combination of the two [sock puppets and bots] can be incredibly powerful because the sock puppet can say one thing, and then the bots can drive that message viral by having thousands or tens of thousands of voices echo it out further. (Davies)

How do we know when information is false? How do we know when we're listening to a sock puppet or a bot? It's actually extremely difficult, especially as the artificial intelligence behind them gets more and more sophisticated. The best answer may be to not like or share information unless we KNOW it's accurate. Social media is so effective at getting people to click, like, and share that that's a tall order for many of us. But it's part of the new reality of listening in the twenty-first century. (It also was forecast in many eerie ways by George Orwell's *1984* and *Animal Farm*, both of which point out specifically how governments can use language to pervert and distort the truth.)

News shows on television and the print media also spread misinformation, sometimes in the very attempt to present a range of views. So concerned are media outlets about appearing balanced that they will put true experts and a public relations spokesperson on the same panel just to air a range of views. Unfortunately, this can elevate a nonexpert to the status of an expert and confuse the issue more than enlighten the audience. This is called a *false equivalence*, and it's a serious impediment to the truth. Veteran teachers must help students recognize the plethora of false equivalences being presented as a way to negate their effects. Some opinions are simply not worth hearing.

Another problem is the language of hate. Racism, misogyny, homophobia, ableism, and bigotry of all kinds should not be listened to—at least not with a sincere, open mind. Such ideas are harmful and hateful. This isn't to say those ideas shouldn't be allowed to have a voice. Freedom of speech is and should remain a foundational value of our democracy. But allowing a voice to be heard and choosing to listen to it closely are two different things. Choosing to listen closely to hatred is not a good idea.

Many educators of color have pointed out that engaging students in simulations and mock debates, for example about slavery or about the motives behind the Holocaust, can cause irreparable damage, especially to students whose heritage is on the receiving end of hatred. Empathy is definitely a good thing. But there are limits to empathy. Nicole Mirra says:

> At the most basic level, we likely can agree that perspectives denigrating or attacking any person or persons on the basis of any identity attributes are not deserving of empathy; however, at a time when it is becoming more and more difficult to separate political positions from judgements of identity (hence the phrase " identity politics"), enforcing even this fundamental rule can become murky. (44)

Further, Mirra draws on Hess and McAvoy in describing the difference between "open" and "settled" issues (qtd. in Mirra). Some ideas and philosophies are *settled*. We need not reopen them. Do we really want students to empathize with racist slave-owners who argued that Black people should be forced to work in inhuman conditions with no freedom? Do we really think it's productive for young people to try to come to a sensitive understanding of why someone might think it's a good idea to systematically imprison, starve, and murder Jewish people? Freedom of speech and education does not mean we must relitigate settled questions in our classes. Instead, we should teach students about why these ideas deserve no hearing and should be confronted forcefully.

In an exchange on Twitter (see Figure 6.3), Tricia Ebarvia explained briefly to Ken why classroom simulations regarding American slavery and similar topics can be wrongheaded.

In our class discussions, it should be made clear that not all views are, in fact, equally valid. Some opinions are not worth listening to, even if it's important that we *hear* them so

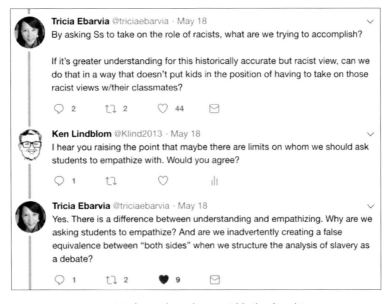

FIGURE 6.3. Twitter exchange between Tricia Ebarvia and Ken.

we know they are out there; there are perspectives with which it is inappropriate to empathize. Determining what those unworthy opinions and perspectives are—especially in an atmosphere of open debate—requires explicit, well-informed critical and ethical thinking. Exactly the kinds of skills we hope students will develop and take from our classes.

MORE ON THE LANGUAGE OF HATE

A school in Lansing, Michigan, recently joined the antibullying Chalkboard Project. For the project, students and staff wrote on small chalkboards words that had been used to make them feel bad about themselves (e.g., *slut*, *fat*, *worthless*); then they posed with the words for photos that were made into posters that hung on the school walls. As reported (Putnam), after a couple of weeks, the chalkboards were covered with blank paper, and school and community members were invited to write counterwords that offered positivity instead of negativity to their peers on the posters: e.g., *helpful*, *friendly*, *nice*. This is a far more effective way to counter bigotry than well-intended but ill-fated simulations of historic prejudice.

In the end, as we teach listening for understanding and empathy, we must also ensure that students develop the critical skills to assert their right not to listen. Just as there are many new doors to open, there are also some doors better kept closed.

CONCLUSION

Every bit as complex and important as reading, critical listening should be a significant part of all English language arts classes. With improving technology, we may even become a more oral-based culture than we are presently. For too long, we have as a field treated listening skills as an add-on. This is shortsighted because our students need high-level critical listening skills to be successful citizens, and our communities will be better places if more people listen to each other. It's not just that we are doing our part in our classrooms to elevate listening to its rightful place in the English curriculum; we are, in a small way, helping to improve the world.

Beyond Your Classroom and Your Students: What Students Need to Know and What They Can Anticipate in Their Futures

One of the most challenging aspects of being a teacher is that a great deal of our skills instruction is geared toward our students' needs for future life and work. For most of us teaching today, our curriculum materials routinely cite the imperative for instruction in "twenty-first-century skills," and there is a real expectation that what we do in the classroom will transmit successfully into future realms of higher education, the workplace, and the community. As daunting as this imperative may be, the expectation is not without precedent, as the classroom has historically been expected to be "porous" and to be fully informed by the world outside school walls. The fact that professional training for teachers and funding for schools often do not support this expectation is routinely left unaddressed, much to the frustration of us as veteran teachers. Thus, through professional development, which may or may not be robust, and professional reading and study, for which teachers are rarely allowed time in our work schedules, we are expected to know and translate "cutting-edge" material in our teaching. In addition, when we consider the rapidity of change in our current age (a rapidity that even the best-funded corporations and entities often struggle to convey to their personnel), the expectation that what we do in the classroom on any given day will have currency in the near or far future is often an overly optimistic, if not an entirely forlorn, hope.

That said, and understanding that the oft-cited and waggish complaint that "the future isn't what it used to be" is somewhat appropriate here, what is our obligation to our students beyond our classroom? Even as we acknowledge the difficulties of the task and the tepid support many of us have to accomplish that task, what can we do to help students as they move beyond us into the world? How does our knowledge of language, listening, and speaking relate to our students' lives beyond us in higher education, in the workplace, and in the community?

LANGUAGE, SPEAKING, AND LISTENING IN HIGHER EDUCATION

College campuses have long been a focus for disputes about communication that is accurate, respectful, and correct. Although it is often satirized in the press, these recurring language concerns can consume campus life and propel students and faculty to reassess and reconsider what is appropriate language (see, for instance, the controversies detailed in Chapter 3 of this book). Often dismissed by the popular press as nothing more important than a fearful adherence to what is "politically correct," these discussions and controversies are ones our students need to be aware of and to which they need to be responsive. Qualities students need to bring to their lives and studies in higher education are:

- ▸ An understanding that new ideas and controversies may be difficult to discuss and resolve and that final consensus is not always possible

- ▸ Active, respectful listening even in tense and difficult discussions

- ▸ Care in addressing all peers and attention to the use of terms for groups; individual pronouns; and pronunciation of others' names

- ▸ Discretion in online presence and awareness that what is tweeted or emailed or forwarded will remain consistently accessible on the internet and linked to the student's name

‣ A demonstrated willingness—even a predisposition—to be forthright and honest in all communications

While none of these attributes is antithetical to the high school and middle school classroom, the stakes can be higher in colleges and universities, and students need to be aware—if not vigilant—that communication standards are different in degree, if not in kind.

LANGUAGE, SPEAKING, AND LISTENING IN THE WORKPLACE

Every workplace has its language mores and protocols as well as, to various extents, its specialized vocabulary. Learning and using these can be essential to success in any job, and paying attention to what is routinely used in communication is important for workplace satisfaction. It is also true, however, that some workplaces are less than friendly to all employees, and awareness of where one would personally draw the line is important. For instance, if there is a consistent use of less than respectful language for certain employees, is that a practice that a new employee should or can mimic? This can include jokes, nicknames, and other kinds of humor that are less funny than an effort to label and divide.

 **MY MOTHER ENTERED** *the workplace in her early forties, in her case by necessity and not by choice, but she absolutely made the best of it, received some basic training for her entry-level job, and quickly rose to head an office and a number of employees. Her intelligence and energy were strong assets, and she needed the money. It was the early 1960s, and despite the occasional unwelcome advances or, conversely, the hostile barbs of men with whom she worked, my mother made a solid, if short, career in the workplace. I spent two summers in her office as a part-time typist and watched her deftly use language to cajole, deflect, and inform both clients and employees, skills that were essential to her*

success at the time as a woman at work. My mother was an empathetic listener, but when she spoke it was decisive and direct. She also consistently conveyed her strong interest in people, and though she was raised in a classist and discriminatory environment, in the workplace she conveyed egalitarian principles.

As the decades moved on, however, such deftness was not always needed, and women and people of color in particular began to push back at the kind of jibes and aggressions my mother routinely endured. Yet my mother's skills remain essential to workplace success. And just recently I was saddened to learn that a distant relative, now in his mid-forties, was fired from his job for inappropriate workplace language. The product of a small southern town and a set of beliefs about who should and should not be accrued respect, this relative unleashed discriminatory language at women one time too many, and his actions had serious consequences. The father of two children and a man who has no interest in moving to a larger city or acquiring a new set of skills, he now faces a degree of economic uncertainty. He is essentially a good person and a hard worker, but what he has deemed acceptable language—and what in my mother's day might well have been ignored or laughed at—has cost him his job.

Ethical values students need to bring to their lives in the workplace are:

▸ Awareness of and sensitivity to how peers and authority figures are addressed in this workplace

▸ Care in using humorous or informal language, especially teasing or sarcastic interactions, with peers and, in particular, with authority figures

▸ Mastery of specialized vocabulary or phrases that pertain to this workplace

I GREW UP IN THE *Bronx, and I lived there until I went away to college at eighteen years old. I had a heavy Bronx accent, as did all my relatives and friends. Once in a debate team event, I lost "speaker points" because I pronounced airbags as "aaahbaaags."*

Now, people often remark on the fact that I have no New York City accent, even though my family still does. Even my loving wife recently said, "I never hear any Bronx accent from you at all. Of course, it may just be that I don't really listen to you."

So why don't I have a Bronx accent?

I attended a college where students from many other areas also went, and NYC accents weren't all that common. When I became an English major and an education minor, my dorm mates decided I shouldn't use "NY-speak," so they began a concerted effort to eliminate my accent. They called me out when I said "huh" instead of "her," "cawfee" instead of "coffee," and "soder" instead of "soda." They teased me unmercifully, but always in fun, and what they really did was simply raise my awareness. I began changing my own pronunciation. I have no doubt that this change in my accent helped me secure a job as a high school English teacher in upstate New York, where a NYC accent might well have caused concern among the job search committee.

I was never angry with my friends; in fact, I was always somewhat grateful to them for raising my language awareness. But, in removing my accent, I now acknowledge that I also lost a part of my identity. The fact that this loss may have had positive professional results says some rather unpleasant things about our culture. And I also think that may be changing. When I hear politicians like Bernie Sanders speak unapologetically with a Brooklyn accent, or even when George W. Bush would say "nuke-u-

ler" rather than "nuke-lee-er," I appreciate it. Regional accents are part of culture and identity. While we learn that some people may interpret our accents as deficits, we should also remember that this is just another form of bigotry.

LANGUAGE, SPEAKING, AND LISTENING IN THE COMMUNITY

The rhetorical concept of *register*—changing the formality of our talk depending on our audience—is never more essential than in the communities in which we live. Students need to be reminded—and many of them already know as they have experienced it deeply—that the use of certain expressions and vocabulary types them in a certain way. The key, we think, is not to be afraid of such typing, but to know that it can be employed as a deliberate, intentional tool. In certain contexts, we want to convey certain class and social attitudes; the same may not be appropriate in other contexts. In this instance, we as teachers are not particularly essential for student success, as the instructors who are best equipped to help young people shape language, speaking, and listening in their community are already in place in their families and extended social circles. What, however, we can do with our students is to reinforce with them the concept of *effective language in relation to a specific audience*, a distinction that, even to this day, often gets lost. In the concern about "correctness," consistently documented in this book, well-meaning teachers can often imply to students that there is only one way to communicate and one ideal audience. This belief is incorrect and will not further our students' success in their lives in their communities. Instead, we must teach them for the world as it is by focusing on how language is authentically used in the real world.

While our students essentially know that a universal definition of correctness is false, many of them will not challenge any teacher on the topic—and if they did, they might well lose. As veteran teachers, we know better and can reinforce with students that success in the community is characterized by:

- ▸ Understanding of varying audiences in the community and adjustment of language, speaking, and listening to that audience

- ▸ Awareness that age and experience, as well as gender identification, socioeconomic status, and race, are also factors in an audience's receptivity

- ▸ Ability to make intentional adjustments to language, speaking, and listening in relation to audience

A NOTE ON MICROAGGRESSIONS

As White people accustomed to authority and power, we have been greatly interested in the recent identification of what is termed *microaggressions*, and we have participated in training sessions regarding the definition and identification of this concept. While we don't believe that any level of conflict between people of unequal status should automatically be called a microaggression—and we have seen the term misused in our own workplaces—the concept and the term bring definition to what many of us have observed and now can label effectively. It also can lend clarity to subtle yet effective language moves that can silence and marginalize people of unequal status who interact on a routine basis. Ken's colleague Robbye Kinkade, a clinical assistant professor at Stony Brook University, teaches workshops on microaggressions, which she calls "papercuts." Anyone would be at least slightly annoyed by a papercut, but get a bunch of them every day and they can be absolute torture. Leila had an experience that demonstrates how this can happen.

SOME TIME AGO I *served for three years on a small civic board, which was a nonprofit directly related to the urban and historic neighborhood in which I lived. At the time, the board was peopled entirely by professional White men and women and the nonprofit's director, a White woman who brought to the task a great deal*

of energy and skill. While the board had been technically integrated for some time, it had been a while since a person of color had actually served, and there was an effort to be more intentionally diverse in the selection of board members. Soon this nonprofit organization nominated, elected, and welcomed to the board a person of color, a successful businessman who was serious about his work for this nonprofit.

Only after the first few monthly board meetings did the White board members come to realize that the director of the nonprofit was uncomfortable with this gentleman's presence. Her strategy was to use a title and his surname, deliberately addressing this man as Mr. Johnson (not his real name), whereas she addressed everyone else on the board by their first name, Leila, Bob, Karen. It may seem, in hindsight, a small thing, but her strategy was clear and discomforting: the director could claim that she was being respectful and appropriate, but it was obvious to me and the other board members that this was a way to distance—isolate?—Charles Johnson from the group. Her behavior was, although the term was not in currency at the time, a microaggression.

At one point, the new board member openly queried the director on her choice of address. In our monthly meetings, we as board members had consistently addressed one another—including our new member—by first name, but the practice had not "taken" with the director. The confrontation appeared to be effective—the director changed her form of address— but the damage was done. Charles had confronted the issue, the board members had supported him, but it was too little, too late. We lost Charles Johnson and his talents soon after when he submitted his resignation. He may well have felt that volunteering on this board was not worth his time. It was our loss and a lost opportunity to be more actively inclusive and welcoming of another's talents, and I worry to this day what more I as an individual could have done.

CONCLUSION

English teachers have, over the decades, maintained that knowledge and mastery of their subject are central to life success. The effective use of language, careful listening, and thoughtful, deliberate speaking are all components of a productive and well-lived life. Today, certainly, language remains central to our nation's discourse, and the ongoing contention between opposing groups largely relies on the choice of language, the careful act of listening, and the employment of speech in the service of a range of ethical goals. Regardless of our political orientation, language, speaking, and listening are premier tools—and weapons.

Equipping our students surely and precisely for what they will encounter over the course of their lives beyond us is not a completely realistic goal; but raising many of the issues as we see them and helping students make informed choices about what words they use, what actions they take, and what influence they accept is part of our responsibility as veteran English teachers. If we are lucky, we will live to see those students take their places in the world and contribute positively and effectively to a better society and a more just world. Their journeys, often taking turns we have yet to imagine, may well be steadier and longer thanks to an enhanced understanding of language, speaking, and listening. And our continuing journeys as veteran teachers may lead us to higher ground thanks to their efforts in the world beyond our classrooms.

NOTES

1. Astute readers may note that some of the ideas in this opening are inspired by David Foster Wallace's *This Is Water: Some Thoughts, Delivered on a Significant Occasion, about Living a Compassionate Life*, which we discuss in Chapter 4.

2. Much of the text in the conclusion of this chapter has appeared in print before; see Leila Christenbury, "The Power to Name."

WORKS CITED

@hfdavis. "Reply to this with a thread about the moment you realized you were using the wrong shade of emoji based on how 'melanated' you see yourself versus how others see you. . . . My friend wants to see something. The friend is me." *Twitter,* 24 Mar. 2019, 12:34 p.m., https://twitter.com/hfdavis/status/1109901393630916608.

@Klind2013. "I hear you raising the point that maybe there are limits on whom we should ask students to empathize with. Would you agree?" *Twitter,* 18 May 2019, 1:40 p.m., https://twitter.com/Klind2013/status/1129849193739239425.

@triciaebarvia. "By asking Ss to take on the role of racists, what are we trying to accomplish? If it's greater understanding for this historically accurate but racist view, can we do that in a way that doesn't put kids in the position of having to take on those racist views w/their classmates?" *Twitter,* 18 May 2019, 1:03 p.m., https://twitter.com/triciaebarvia/status/1129840028237139968.

———. "Yes. There is a difference between understanding and empathizing. Why are we asking students to empathize? And are we inadvertently creating a false equivalence between "both sides" when we structure the analysis of slavery as a debate?" *Twitter,* 18 May 2019, 1:41 p.m., https://twitter.com/triciaebarvia/status/1129849566537367553.

Associated Press Stylebook, The. Associated Press, 2018.

Barnwell, Paul. "My Students Don't Know How to Have a Conversation: 'Students' Reliance on Screens for Communication Is Detracting—and Distracting—from Their Engagement in Real-Time Talk.'" *The Atlantic,* 22 Apr. 2014, https://www.theatlantic.com/education/archive/2014/04/my-students-dont-know-how-to-have-a-conversation/360993/.

Bartlett, Tom. "A Professor Has Long Used a Racial Slur in Class Epithet in Class to Teach Free-Speech Law. No More, He Says." *Chronicle of Higher Education,* 7 Mar. 2019, https://www.chronicle.com/article/A-Professor-Has-Long-Used-a/245838.

"Before Public Speaking. . ." *TED Recommends,* https://www.ted.com/playlists/226/before_public_speaking.

Bowles, Nellie. "Human Contact Is Now a Luxury Good: Screens Used to Be for the Elite. Now Avoiding Them Is a Status Symbol." *The New York Times Sunday Review,* 23 Mar. 2019, https://www.nytimes.com/2019/03/23/sunday-review/human-contact-luxury-screens.html.

Britton, James. *Language and Learning.* U of Miami P, 1970.

Brownell, Cassie J., and Jon M. Wargo. "(Re)educating the Senses to Multicultural Communities: Prospective Teachers Using Digital Media and Sonic Cartography to Listen for Culture." *Multicultural Education Review,* vol. 9, no. 3, 24 Jul. 2017, pp. 201–14.

Bryson, Bill. *The Mother Tongue: English and How It Got That Way.* Perennial, 2001.

Chicago Manual of Style, The. 17th ed., U of Chicago P, 2017.

Chira, Susan. "The Universal Phenomenon of Men Interrupting Women." *The New York Times,* 14 Jun. 2017, https://www.nytimes.com/2017/06/14/business/women-sexism-work-huffington-kamala-harris.html.

Chism, Sherwanda. "Respectful Talk." *Teaching Channel,* https://www.teachingchannel.org/video/speaking-respectfully-nea.

Christenbury, Leila. "NCTE and the Shaping of American Literacy Education." *Reading the Past, Writing the Future: A Century of American Literacy Education and the National Council of Teachers of English,* edited by Erika Lindemann, National Council of Teachers of English, 2010, pp. 1–52.

———. "The Power to Name." *English Journal,* vol. 108, no. 1, 2018, pp. 16–17.

Christenbury, Leila, and Patricia P. Kelly. *Questioning: A Path to Critical Thinking.* ERIC Clearinghouse on Reading and Communication Skills and National Council of Teachers of English, 1983.

Christenbury, Leila, and Ken Lindblom. "The Craft of Questioning." *Making the Journey: Being and Becoming a Teacher of English Language Arts.* 4th ed., Heinemann, 2016, pp. 334–57.

———. *Continuing the Journey: Becoming a Better Teacher of Literature and Informational Texts.* National Council of Teachers of English, 2017.

Clark, Eve V., and Herbert H. Clark. "When Nouns Surface as Verbs." *Language,* vol. 55, no. 4, 1979, pp. 767–811. DOI: 10.2307/412745.

Coffee-Shop Background Noise Generator. Café Restaurant, https://mynoise.net/NoiseMachines/cafeRestaurantNoiseGenerator.php.

Connors, Sean P., and P. L. Thomas, guest editors. "Visible Teaching: Open Doors as Resistance." *English Journal* Focus Issue, vol. 106, no. 2, 2016.

Council of Writing Program Administrators, National Council of Teachers of English, and National Writing Project. *Framework for Success in Postsecondary Writing.* Jan. 2011, http://wpacouncil.org/files/framework-for-success-postsecondary-writing.pdf.

Crystal, David. *Spell It Out: The Curious, Enthralling, and Extraordinary Story of English Spelling.* St. Martin's Press, 2012.

Davies, Dave. "The 'Weaponization' of Social Media—And Its Real-World Consequences." *National Public Radio,* 9 Oct. 2018, https://www.npr.org/2018/10/09/655824435/the-weaponization-of-social-media-and-its-real-world-consequences.

Dean, Deborah. "*EJ* in Focus: Shifting Perspectives about Grammar: Changing What and How We Teach." *English Journal,* vol. 100, no. 4, 2011, pp. 20–26.

"Debrief Circles." *Teaching Channel,* https://www.teachingchannel.org/video/students-reflect-on-learning-exl.

Delpit, Lisa. *Other People's Children: Cultural Conflict in the Classroom.* New Press, 2006.

DiAngelo, Robin. *White Fragility: Why It's So Hard for White People to Talk about Racism.* Beacon Press, 2018.

Dunn, Patricia A., and Ken Lindblom. *Grammar Rants: How a Backstage Tour of Writing Complaints Can Help Students Make Informed, Savvy Choices about Their Writing.* Boynton/Cook, 2011.

Edublogs. "50 Ideas for Student Created Podcasts." n.d., https://www.theedublogger.com/files/2018/04/50-Ideas-for-Student-Created-Podcasts-1ae2ib7-2lumdoa.pdf.

Elbow, Peter. "The Believing Game—Methodological Believing." *The Journal of the Assembly for Expanded Perspectives on Learning,* vol. 14, 2008, https://scholarworks.umass.edu/eng_faculty_pubs/5.

Eligon, John. "Speaking Black Dialect in Courtrooms Can Have Striking Consequences." *The New York Times,* 25 Jan. 2019, https://www.nytimes.com/2019/01/25/us/black-dialect-courtrooms.html.

Filkins, Scott. "Conducting Inner-Outer Circle Discussions." *ReadWriteThink,* http://www.readwritethink.org/professional-development/strategy-guides/conducting-inner-outer-circle-31227.html.

Fleming, Crystal M. *How to Be Less Stupid about Race: On Racism, White Supremacy, and the Racial Divide.* Beacon Press, 2018.

Fogarty, Mignon, Grammar Girl. "Based Off versus Based On." *Quick and Dirty Tips: Do Things Better,* 13 Nov. 2014, https://www.quickanddirtytips.com/education/grammar/based-off-versus-based-on.

Frost, Aja. "68 Memorable Questions for Establishing and Building Rapport with Customers." *HubSpot.* Originally published 5 June 2019, 4:11:37 p.m., updated 26 Aug. 2019, https://blog.hubspot.com/service/rapport-building-questions.

Fulfilling the American Dream: Liberal Education and the Future of Work: Selected Findings from Online Surveys of Business Executives and Hiring Managers. Association of American Colleges and Universities, 2018, https://www.aacu.org/sites/default/files/files/LEAP/2018EmployerResearchReport.pdf.

Garner, Bryan A. *Garner's Modern American Usage: The Authority on Grammar, Usage, and Style.* 3rd ed., Oxford UP, 2009.

———. *Garner's Modern American Usage: The Authority on Grammar, Usage, and Style.* 4th ed., Oxford UP, 2016.

Gay, Geneva. *Culturally Responsive Teaching: Theory, Research, and Practice.* 3rd ed., Teachers College P, 2018.

Gilmore, Barry. *Speaking Volumes: How to Get Students Discussing Books—And Much More.* Heinemann, 2006.

Goering, Chris. *Big Engine.* Dreaming Dust, 2016.

Goering, Christian Z., and Paul Thomas, editors. *Critical Media Literacy and Fake News in Post-Truth America.* Brill Sense, 2018.

Gonzales, Jennifer. "The Fisheye Syndrome: Is Every Student Really Participating?" *Cult of Pedagogy,* 25 Sept. 2013, https://www.cultofpedagogy.com/fisheye/.

———. "The Big List of Class Discussion Strategies." *Cult of Pedagogy,* 15 Oct. 2015, https://www.cultofpedagogy.com/speaking-listening-techniques/.

Hess, Diana E., and Paula McAvoy. *The Political Classroom: Evidence and Ethics in Democratic Education.* Routledge, 2014.

Hess, Karin K. "Cognitive Rigor Matrix." 2009, https://static.pdesas.org/content/documents/M1-Slide_22_DOK_Hess_Cognitive_Rigor.pdf.

Hitchings, Henry. *The Language Wars: A History of Proper English.* Picador, 2012.

Holcombe, Madeline. "Gucci Apologizes after Social Media Users Say Sweater Resembles Blackface." *CNN.* 8 Feb. 2019, https://www.cnn.com/2019/02/07/us/gucci-blackface-sweater/index.html.

Indiana University Center for Innovative Teaching and Learning. "Discussion Techniques for Active Learning: Dictionary of Methods and Strategies." n.d., https://citl.indiana.edu/files/pdf/Discussion_Techniques_2010.pdf.

Inoue, Asao B. "How Do We Language So People Stop Killing Each Other, or What Do We Do about White Language Supremacy?" Chair's Address at Conference on College Composition and Communication Annual Convention, Pittsburgh, PA, 14 Mar. 2019, https://www.youtube.com/watch?v=brPGTewcDYY&feature=youtu.be&fbclid=IwAR3gH7BNoBfPOoZWPcyBs5DEAer3apEuul4SckIDc940cmZ1fw7ekks8IT8 and https://docs.google.com/presentation/d/1C2gGz2SEzt8fcb1WdsGPjWkQ98AC-8onTY-zeSX5UPg/edit#slide=id.g3fd0a840bc_0_179.

Johns, Tony. "Truthiness." *Urban Dictionary.* 9 Jan. 2006, http://www.urbandictionary.com.

Johnson, Steven. "Colleges Lose a 'Stunning' 651 Foreign-Language Programs in 3 Years." *Chronicle of Higher Education,* 22 Jan. 2019, https://www.chronicle.com/article/Colleges-Lose-a-Stunning-/245526.

Kay, Matthew R. *Not Light but Fire: How to Lead Meaningful Race Conversations in the Classroom.* Stenhouse, 2018.

Keely, Karen A. "Dangerous Words: Recognizing the Power of Language by Researching Derogatory Terms." *English Journal,* vol. 100, no. 4, 2011, pp. 55–60.

Lapp, Diane, Douglas Fisher, and Nancy Frey, editors. "Speaking and Listening." *Voices from the Middle* Focus Issue, vol. 22, no. 1, 2014.

Lenhart, Amanda, Aaron Smith, Monica Anderson, Maeve Duggan, and Andrew Perrin. "Teens, Technology & Friendship: Video Games, Social Media and Mobile Phones Play an Integral Role in How Teens Meet and Interact with Friends." Pew Research Center, 6 Aug. 2015, https://www.pewresearch.org/wp-content/uploads/sites/9/2015/08/Teens-and-Friendships-FINAL2.pdf.

Leonard, Sterling Andrus. *The Doctrine of Correctness in English Usage, 1700–1800.* U of Wisconsin P, 1929. University of Wisconsin Studies in Language and Literature No. 25, https://archive.org/stream/doctrineofcorrecooleon/doctrineofcorrecooleon_djvu.tx.

LeslieKnopeRocks. *Parks and Recreation* Deleted Scene—Park Safety 2." *YouTube,* 6 May 2010, https://www.youtube.com/watch?v=53xMff0a3Ec.

Lindblom, Ken, editor. "Beyond Grammar: The Richness of English Language." *English Journal* Focus Issue, vol. 100, no. 4, 2011.

Lindblom, Ken, and Leila Christenbury. *Continuing the Journey 2: Becoming a Better Teacher of Authentic Writing.* National Council of Teachers of English, 2018.

Lindblom, Kenneth, William Banks, and Rise Quay. "Mid-Nineteenth-Century Writing Instruction at Illinois State Normal University: Credentials, Correctness, and the Rise of a Teaching Class." *Local Histories: Reading the Archives of Composition,* edited by Patricia Donahue and Gretchen Flesher Moon, U of Pittsburgh P, 2007, pp. 94–114.

Lorenz, Taylor. "Teens Are Protesting In-Class Presentations: Some Students Say Having to Speak in Front of the Class Is an Unreasonable Burden for Those with Anxiety and Are Demanding Alternative Options." *The Atlantic,* 12 Sept. 2018, https://www.theatlantic.com/education/archive/2018/09/teens-think-they-shouldnt-have-to-speak-in-front-of-the-class/570061/.

Mayo Clinic Staff. "Being Assertive: Reduce Stress, Communicate Better." *Mayo Clinic,* 9 May 2017, https://www.mayoclinic.org/healthy-lifestyle/stress-management/in-depth/assertive/art-20044644.

McCann, Thomas M., Larry R. Johannessen, Elizabeth Kahn, and Joseph M. Flanagan. *Talking in Class: Using Discussion to Enhance Teaching and Learning.* National Council of Teachers of English, 2006.

McGregor, Tanny. *Ink and Ideas: Sketchnotes for Engagement, Comprehension, and Thinking.* Heinemann, 2019.

Mckesson, DeRay. "'I learned hope the hard way': On the Early Days of Black Lives Matter." *The Guardian,* 12 Apr. 2019, https://www.theguardian.com/world/2019/apr/12/black-lives-matter-deray-mckesson-ferguson-protests.

Michael, Ali. *Raising Race Questions: Whiteness and Inquiry in Education.* Teachers College P, 2015.

Miller, sj, editor. *Teaching, Affirming, and Recognizing Trans* and Gender Creative Youth: A Queer Literacy Framework.* Palgrave Macmillan, 2016.

Mirra, Nicole. *Educating for Empathy: Literacy Learning and Civic Engagement.* Teachers College P and National Writing Project, 2018.

Morrison, Toni. *The Source of Self-Regard: Selected Essays, Speeches, and Meditations.* Alfred A. Knopf, 2019.

National Board for Professional Teaching Standards. *English Language Arts Standards for Teachers of Students Ages 11–18+.* 3rd ed., 2014, http://www.nbpts.org/wp-content/uploads/EAYA-ELA.pdf.

National Council of Teachers of English. "NCTE/NCATE Standards for Initial Preparation of Teachers of Secondary English Language Arts, Grades 7–12." Oct. 2012, http://www.ncte.org/library/NCTEFiles/Groups/CEE/NCATE/ApprovedStandards_111212.pdf.

———. *Statement on Anti-Racism to Support Teaching and Learning.* 11 Jul. 2018. Accessed 31 May 2019, http://www2.ncte.org/statement/antiracisminteaching/.

———. *Statement on Gender and Language.* 25 Oct. 2018. Accessed 30 Jan. 2019, https://www2.ncte.org/statement/genderfairuseoflang/.

———. *Students' Right to Their Own Language.* 17 Apr. 1974, http://www.ncte.org/library/NCTEFiles/Groups/CCCC/NewSRTOL.pdf?_ga=2.97249879.996580005.1567603750-1813913100.1547753429.

National Council of Teachers of English and International Reading Association. *Standards for the English Language Arts.* NCTE and IRA, 2012, http://www.ncte.org/standards/ncte-ira.

National Science Foundation. "Enough with the Lecturing: Active Learning Improves Grades, Reduces Failure among Undergrads in STEM." *National Science Foundation.* 12 May 2014, https://nsf.gov/news/news_summ.jsp?cntn_id=131403&org=NSF&from=news.

New York State Education Department. *New York State Next Generation Learning Standards for Literacy in History/Social Studies, Science and Technical Subjects, Grades 6–12.* 2017, http://www.nysed.gov/common/nysed/files/programs/curriculum-instruction/nys-next-generation-literacy-standards-grades-6-12.pdf.

———. *New York State Next Generation English Language Arts Learning Standards, Grade P–12.* 2017, http://www.nysed.gov/common/nysed/files/programs/curriculum-instruction/nys-next-generation-ela-standards.pdf.

Nichols, Maria. *Building Bigger Ideas: A Process for Teaching Purposeful Talk.* Heinemann, 2019.

Nilsen, Don F. "Humor in American Pop Language" [PowerPoint]. 2017.

Nilsen, Aileen Pace, and Don L. F. Nilsen. *The Language of Humor: An Introduction.* Cambridge UP, 2019.

NPR. "Starting Your Podcast: A Guide for Students." *NPR,* 15 Nov. 2018, https://www.npr.org/2018/11/15/662070097/starting-your-podcast-a-guide-for-students#toolbox.

Oliveros, Pauline. "The Difference between Hearing and Listening." TEDx Talks. *YouTube,* 12 Nov. 2015, https://www.youtube.com/watch?v=_QHfOuRrJB8.

Oluo, Ijeoma. *So You Want to Talk about Race.* Seal Press, 2018.

Orwell, George. "Politics and the English Language." *The Collected Essays, Journalism, and Letters of George Orwell,* edited by Sonial Orwell and Ian Angus, vol. 4, pp. 127–40, Harcourt, 1968. Accessed at faculty.washington.edu/rsoder/EDLPS579/HonorsOrwell PoliticsEnglishLanguage.pdf.

Osei, Zipporah. "Do Racial Epithets Have Any Place in the Classroom? A Professor's Suspension Fuels That Debate." *Chronicle of Higher Education,* 8 Feb. 2019, https://www.chronicle.com/article/Do-Racial-Epithets-Have-Any/245662.

Owens, Cassie. "Are Philly Court Reporters Accurate with Black Dialect? Study: Not Really." *The Philadelphia Inquirer,* 22 Jan. 2019, https://www.inquirer.com/news/court-reporter-stenographer-african-american-english-aave-philly-transcript-study-20190122.html.

Pariser, Eli. "Beware Online 'Filter Bubbles.'" TED Talk, Mar. 2011, https://www.ted.com/talks/eli_pariser_beware_online_filter_bubbles?language=en.

"Poetry Visualization: Draw What You Hear." *Teaching Channel,* https://www.teachingchannel.org/video/teaching-poetry-with-visualization.

Pullum, Geoff. "Can a Word Capture the Zeitgeist of a Year? No. Maybe. Yes It Can." *Chronicle of Higher Education,* 6 Jan. 2019, https://www.chronicle.com/article/Can-a-Word-Capture-the/245419.

Putnam, Judy. "Ugly. Fat. Worthless. Slut. Bath High School Project Puts Hurtful Words on the Walls." *Lansing State Journal,* 12 Dec. 2018, https://www.lansingstatejournal.com/story/opinion/columnists/judy-putnam/2018/12/12/bath-high-school-michigan-chalkboard-project-school-bullying/2286990002/?fbclid=IwARovnmnRKrvH6ySMZDxw2Ll6DEJOrlIu2RNjzlPvEzed4qQ8CR_iT5sF4Ww.

Ramey, Jessie B. "A Note from Your Colleagues with Hearing Loss: Just Use a Microphone Already." *The Chronicle of Higher Education.* 20 Mar. 2019, https://www.chronicle.com/article/a-note-from-your-colleagues/245916?fbclid=IwAR3wmUPiwNLrkWoe7_KGmcyOfrmNIMyrVMujtjjw7jlX24HLQE19GdMh9Nw.

ReadWriteThink. "Podcasts: The Nuts and Bolts of Creating Podcasts." *ReadWriteThink,* n.d., http://www.readwritethink.org/classroom-resources/printouts/podcasts-nuts-bolts-creating-30311.html.

"Respectful Talk." *Teaching Channel,* https://www.teachingchannel.org/video/speaking-respectfully-nea.

Reynolds, Garr. *Presentation Zen Design: A Simple Visual Approach to Presenting in Today's World.* New Riders, 2014.

———. *Presentation Zen: Simple Ideas on Presentation Design and Delivery.* 2nd ed. New Riders, 2013.

Richmond Times-Dispatch. "Editorial: Nouns Can't Act!" 17 Jan. 2019.

Richmond, Kia Jane. *Mental Illness in Young Adult Literature: Exploring Real Struggles through Fictional Characters.* Libraries Unlimited, 2019.

Rodríguez, R. Joseph. "History and Repetition: Removing the Cloaks for Socially Just Practices." Guest Post: Dr. R. Joseph Rodríguez for #31DaysIBPOC. *Dr. Kimberly N. Parker.* 6 May 2019, https://drkimparker.org/2019/05/06/guest-post-dr-r-joseph-rodriguez-for-31daysibpoc/.

Rogers, Carl R. "Empathetic: An Unappreciated Way of Being." *The Counseling Psychologist*, vol. 5, no. 2, 1975, pp. 2–11.

———. *On Becoming a Person: A Therapist's View of Psychotherapy.* Houghton Mifflin, 1961.

Schuster, Edgar H. *Breaking the Rules: Liberating Writers through Innovative Grammar Instruction.* Heinemann, 2003.

Searing, Linda. "Sexting Is Increasingly Common for Teens." *Washington Post*, 3 Mar. 2018, https://www.washingtonpost.com/national/health-science/sexting-is-increasingly-common-for-teens/2018/03/02/8e60a236-1d63-11e8-9de1-147dd2df3829_story.html?utm_term=.e6baadcb4147.

Singer, P. W., and Emerson T. Brooking. *LikeWar: The Weaponization of Social Media.* Houghton Mifflin Harcourt, 2018.

Smitherman-Donaldson, Geneva. "Discriminatory Discourse on Afro-American Speech." *Discourse and Discrimination,* edited by Geneva Smitherman-Donaldson and Teun A. van Dijk, Wayne State UP, 1988, pp. 144–75.

"Speak Up: Responding to Everyday Bigotry." *Southern Poverty Law Center,* 26 Jan. 2015, https://www.splcenter.org/20150125/speak-responding-everyday-bigotry.

Steineke, Nancy. *Assessment Live! 10 Real-Time Ways for Kids to Show What They Know—and Meet the Standards.* Heinemann, 2009.

Stone, Geoffrey R., and Lee C. Bollinger, editors. *The Free Speech Century.* Oxford UP, 2018.

Stuart, Dave Jr. *A Non-Freaked Out Guide to Teaching the Common Core: Using the 32 Literacy Anchor Standards to Develop College- and Career-Ready Students.* Jossey-Bass, 2014.

Sue, Derald Wing. "Microaggressions: More Than Just Race: Can Microaggressions Be Directed at Women or Gay People?" *Psychology Today,* 17 Nov. 2010, https://www.psychologytoday.com/us/blog/microaggressions-in-everyday-life/201011/microaggressions-more-just-race.

Sykes, Wanda. *Wanda Sykes: Not Normal.* Netflix, May 2019.

Tatum, Beverly Daniel. *Why Are All the Black Kids Sitting Together in the Cafeteria? And Other Conversations about Race.* Revised and updated ed., Basic Books, 2017.

Tchudi, Stephen. "Teaching Language." *Reading the Past, Writing the Future: A Century of American Literacy Education and the National Council of Teachers of English,* edited by Erika Lindemann, National Council of Teachers of English, 2010, pp. 125–69.

"Thumbs Up! Signals to Encourage Active Listening." *Teaching Channel,* https://www.teachingchannel.org/video/teaching-strategy-active-listening.

Vuong, Ocean. *On Earth We're Briefly Gorgeous.* Penguin, 2019.

Wallace, David Foster. *This Is Water: Some Thoughts, Delivered on a Significant Occasion, about Living a Compassionate Life.* Little, Brown, 2009.

Wargo, Jon M. "#SoundingOutMySilence: Reading a LGBTQ Youth's Sonic Cartography as Multimodal (Counter)Storytelling." *Journal of Adolescent & Adult Literacy,* vol. 62, no. 1, pp. 13–23, https://ila.onlinelibrary.wiley.com/doi/epdf/10.1002/jaal.752.

Weiss, Suzannah. "How to Respond to Manterrupting, Because Yes, It's Actually a Thing." *Bustle,* 27 Feb. 2017, https://www.bustle.com/p/how-to-respond-to-manterrupting-because-yes-its-actually-a-thing-40916.

Whitman, Walt. *Walt Whitman's* Leaves of Grass. 150th anniversary ed., edited by David S. Reynolds, Oxford UP, 2005.

"Words of the Year." *American Dialect Society,* https://www.americandialect.org/woty.

Young, Vershawn Ashanti, Rusty Barrett, Y'Shanda Young-Rivera, and Kim Brian Lovejoy. *Other People's English: Code-Meshing, Code-Switching, and African American Literacy.* Teachers College P, 2014.

Zimmer, Ben. "On Language: Truthiness." *New York Times Magazine,* 13 Oct. 2010.

INDEX

AUTHORS

KEN LINDBLOM is professor of English, former director of the English Teacher Education Program, and former dean of the School of Professional Development at Stony Brook University, where he teaches courses in English teacher education, rhetoric, and literature. He started as a high school English teacher at Columbia High School in East Greenbush, New York, in 1988. A member of NCTE since 1989, Lindblom was editor of *English Journal* from 2008 to 2013. He is coauthor of four other books about teaching English and author of more than two dozen articles, book chapters, and peer-reviewed blog posts on the subject. His tenth-grade sense of humor wins him equal numbers of friends and enemies, which is better odds than he deserves. He can be contacted at kenneth.lindblom@stonybrook.edu and @klind2013.

LEILA CHRISTENBURY is Commonwealth Professor of English Education at Virginia Commonwealth University, Richmond (Emerita), where she taught English methods, young adult literature, applied English linguistics, and the teaching of writing. A past president of NCTE and a past editor of *English Journal*, her research has been recognized by the David H. Russell Award for Distinguished Research in the Teaching of English; the James N. Britton Award for Inquiry in English Language Arts; and the Edward B. Fry Book Award for Outstanding Contributions to Literacy Research. An active member of NCTE for more than forty years, she has taught in Virginia schools and universities for most of her career. She is the author, coauthor, or editor of fifteen books and the author of approximately 100 chapters and articles on the teaching of English. She is currently an archival researcher at the state Library of Virginia, where she is working on biographies of Virginia suffrage leaders and Reconstruction legislators. She can be contacted at lchriste@vcu.edu and leilachristenbury@gmail.com.

FROM THE TEACHERS' LOUNGE CONTRIBUTORS

SYDNEY G. BRYAN teaches high school English in Brentwood School District, the largest suburban school district in New York State. She previously taught in New York City public schools as well as Stony Brook University's Freedom School. She graduated with her BA in English with a minor in Africana Studies and is currently pursuing an MA in English.

KELLY BYRNE BULL is associate professor at Notre Dame of Maryland University, where she teaches courses in literacy, language, and culture. Bull works with local Baltimore area schools to provide professional development for educators. Her scholarship has been published in *English Journal, The ALAN Review*, and *Theory Into Practice*, as well as in numerous book chapters on adolescent literacy.

TRICIA EBARVIA is an English teacher at a public high school in Pennsylvania. Her roles include Pennsylvania Writing and Literature Project co-director, Heinemann Fellow, and #DisruptTexts co-founder—but above all, Ebarvia is an advocate for literacy instruction rooted in equity and liberation. In her work with the Educator Collaborative, she provides professional development on topics including reading and writing workshop, digital literacies, antibias and antiracist pedagogy, and curriculum design.

CHRISTIAN Z. GOERING is professor of English education at the University of Arkansas and currently serves as director of the Northwest Arkansas Writing Project and chair of the English Language Arts Teacher Educators (ELATE) of NCTE. Goering has released two albums as a singer-songwriter and frequently works in classrooms helping adolescents write original songs. In 2018 his coedited book, *Critical Media Literacy and Fake News in Post Truth America*, was awarded a 2019 Divergent Award for Excellence in 21st Century Literacies Research.

SHARONICA NELSON is a faculty member in secondary English education and co-director of the Red Mountain Writing Project at the University of Alabama at Birmingham. She teaches English language arts methods, young adult literature, and classroom management. Her research interests include urban education, literacy pedagogy, and teacher leadership and professional development. A former secondary English teacher, Nelson is proud of her many years of classroom teaching experience.

MOLLY S. POTAS's teaching career began in an alternative school, where she learned classroom management and the value of a low teacher-to-student ratio while adopting the teaching philosophy of quality over quantity in student education. As she struggled with a major learning disability in school (dyslexia), Potas found that it is critical to show students how they can turn their greatest weakness into their greatest strength. In 2002 she began working at a small K–12 rural school, where she has instructed grades 7–12 English for the past seventeen years, coaches middle school and high school track, and sponsors Wyoming History Day. She also teaches English part-time at Northwest Community College while being a full-time mom and wife.

KIA JANE RICHMOND is a professor of English at Northern Michigan University, where she directs the English education program. She was selected as the recipient of her university's Excellence in Teaching Award in 2014. An active member of NCTE, ELATE, and the Michigan Council of Teachers of English (MCTE), she was awarded the Charles Carpenter Fries Award for Excellence in Teaching/Mentoring by MCTE in 2015. In 2019 she authored *Mental Illness in Young Adult Literature: Exploring Real Struggles through Fictional Characters.*

JANA L. RIECK has a master's in education (teaching and learning) from St. Mary's University in Winona, Minnesota, and a master's in English education from her undergraduate alma mater, Southwest Minnesota State in Marshall. She started her teaching career in a small district of fewer than 500 students but since 1997 has been teaching in Minnesota's largest high school, Champlin Park High School, which serves approximately 3,000 students each year. She is on the executive board of the Minnesota Writing & English Conference (MnWE) serving as the communications coordinator. Rieck is active in social justice, personally and professionally, and literacy. She lives by two guiding quotes: "Well-behaved women seldom make history" (Laurel Thatcher Ulrich) and "The most common way people give up their POWER is by thinking they don't have any" (Alice Walker).

R. JOSEPH RODRÍGUEZ is a literacy educator and researcher in the High Plains and Hill Country of Texas. He is the author of *Enacting Adolescent Literacies across Communities: Latino/a Scribes and Their Rites* (2017), *Teaching Culturally Sustaining and Inclusive Young Adult Literature: Critical Perspectives and Conversations* (2019), and articles in academic journals. Rodríguez has taught English and Spanish language arts in public schools, community colleges, and universities. He serves as coeditor of *English Journal.* Catch him virtually @escribescribe.

MARTHA SANDVEN is a teacher, mentor, and playwright. She graduated with a BS in speech from Northwestern University, earned a master's degree in theater/film from the University of Kansas, and completed a secondary English MAT at the University of Arkansas. Her recognitions include a Point of Light Award (President Bill Clinton), Mentor Teacher of the Year (University of Arkansas), Above and Beyond (Fayetteville Chamber of Commerce), Recognition of Outstanding Achievement (Fayetteville Board of Education), Teacher of the Year (Ramay Junior High), and Outstanding Alumni in Education (University of Arkansas). She is a National Board Certified Teacher in English language arts/early adolescence.

BRIAN SZTABNIK teaches Advanced Placement English Literature and Composition as well as English 12 at Miller Place High School. He also serves as the school's varsity basketball coach. Stzabnik is the creator of *Talks with Teachers*, a top education podcast on iTunes, as well as an award-winning blogger for Edutopia. He serves as the College Board advisor for AP Literature and Composition and serves on its Test Development Committee. In 2018 he was a finalist for the New York State Teacher of the Year.

PETER S. WILLIS has wandered through journalism, law, and education since the early 1990s and still hasn't decided what he wants to be when he grows up. He has taught secondary English, journalism, photojournalism, and creative writing classes for almost twenty years. He is currently completing a PhD in education at Virginia Commonwealth University, Richmond.

This book was typeset in Calluna and Saira by Barbara Frazier.

Typefaces used on the cover include Joe Hand 2, Galaxie Polaris, and Gill Sans MT.

The book was printed on 50-lb. White Offset paper by Seaway Printing Company, Inc.